I MAY SMELL LIKE BACON
BUT I HAVEN'T OINKED YET

Richard Allen Warner, Captain USMC (ret.)

Written by:
Galen B. Conrardy

ISBN 978-1-64471-844-5 (Paperback)
ISBN 978-1-64471-845-2 (Digital)

Covenant Books, Inc.
11661 Hwy 707
Murrells Inlet, SC 29576
www.covenantbooks.com

PREFACE

I have been interested in having my life's story told for over fifteen years. I wanted it to chronicle the trials, tribulations, and triumphs of my life as I recalled them. I've been obsessed with having my biography written ever since I read my uncle's biography entitled *Technocrat*, that was published in 1996.

I was very fortunate to have accidentally met my future biographer at a Village Inn Restaurant some nine months ago in Colorado Springs, Colorado. I'm afraid I may have enticed him to write my biography because of the title I wanted for the book, *I May Smell like Bacon, but I Haven't Oinked Yet*, which he said intrigued him. I thank God that he has stayed the course with me. We would meet for several hours once a week, where we would go over what he had written and then determine what the next couple of chapters would entail. He was constantly on my case to "*stay focused*," as he discovered that I have a bad habit of jumping all over the place in my recollections. He often refers to me as Br'er Rabbit.

This gentleman's name is Galen B. Conrardy. He is a retired teacher/coach. He is also a published author, having written an autobiography about his youth growing up on a farm in Western Kansas in the '40s and '50s entitled *Growing Up with Roy*.

Acknowledgments

There have been some really wonderful people who have been instrumental in shaping my life.

First of all, my family: my mother, Cynthia Warner; my father, Harold Warner, PhD; my sister, Nancy Collins (deceased); my stepbrothers and sisters, Robert (Bobby) Warner, William (Billy) Warner (deceased), Betty Stiles (deceased); and Alex Brooker and Susan Brooker.

Also, thanks to two very special ladies, Druwanda Joan Woolam Warner and Erika Erna Krey Rozak.

And to my children, Devin and Daree, whose lives I was privileged to be a part of during their growing-up years. I miss you.

In addition, I wish to thank Dr. Bill Stone, who is the chief of nephology at the VA Medical Center in Nashville, Tennessee; Dr. Frank Schlichter, a retired plastic surgeon who now resides in Bartow, Florida; and Dr. Rainer Kroll, who is a licensed lawyer and a professor of the German language and lives in Sarasota, Florida.

To all of you, I owe a great sense of gratitude, and I will be forever in your debt.

—Richard Allen Warner, Captain USMC (ret.)

1

CHARLIE PIG SAVES A LIFE

Fatigue was showing on Richard A. Warner's face as he eased the semi eighteen-wheeler into the familiar Truck Stop of America in Branford, Connecticut. It was three o'clock in the morning, and not many trucks were around. He worked for two trucking companies and had just logged eighteen hours of continuous driving. As he stepped down from the rig, he rubbed his eyes and did a brief stretching routine to limber up his stiff joints and aching muscles. Slowly he made his way toward the truckers' showers located in the rear of the building. Richard hadn't showered in two days, and he was hoping a nice long shower would not only cleanse his body but also revive his state of awareness. Driving a big rig required a high degree of alertness, which he knew he was currently lacking.

The long shower stall featured six showerheads in order to handle the trucker traffic. At this time of the morning, Richard had the stall to himself. He quickly shed his smelly clothes and shoes and walked carefully to the nearest shower spigot. The rush of the luke-warm water splashed on his face and shoulders.

"Oh, this feels so good," he exclaimed.

Suddenly a pain shot up his left arm and shoulder. Before he could react, he fell in a heap on the concrete floor. A heavy weight seemed to be pressing on his chest area. He tried crying out for help, but to no avail—no one was nearby. Although he was in excruciating pain, he was able to crawl sideways to the wall where his clothes were. Somehow with his back against the wall, he managed to pull on his trousers. With much effort, he stood with the wall acting as his crutch and slowly staggered to the restaurant area of the truck stop.

"What's the matter?" a startled employee inquired.

"Call for a meat wagon, I'm having a heart attack!"

Within minutes, an ambulance with siren blaring and red lights flashing arrived. As Richard was being strapped onto the gurney and loaded into the ambulance, the head EMT inquired of Richard what hospital he wanted to be taken to.

"Whatever you think is best." Richard grimaced.

"I would recommend the University of Connecticut's Medical Center. They are renowned at helping patients in your condition."

"Good, let's do it!"

Dr. Stephen E. Possick was dressed in his surgical gear waiting for a heart patient to arrive from New Haven when the EMTs ushered Richard into the emergency room. The on-duty nurse informed Richard that there would be several minutes before the next available surgeon reported for duty. Fortunately, a call from New Haven informed the staff that there would be a major delay in the arrival of the scheduled patient. Dr. Stephen E. Possick quickly assessed Richard's critical situation and ordered him to be wheeled into surgery immediately.

Seven hours later, Richard awoke dazed in the hospital's recovery room. Within minutes, Dr. Stephen E. Possick stopped by to check on his patient. "Well, my good man, we had to perform a double bypass procedure on the lower half of your heart. Unfortunately, the upper half of your heart is relatively useless. With proper care and exercise, I think you can lead a useful life. However, at this point in time, one of my big concerns is your lungs. They are black in appearance. Do you smoke three packs of cigarettes a day?"

"No, sir, I haven't smoked since I was twenty-nine years old!"

"Well then, what do you do for a living?"

"I drive semi-trucks around the country delivering goods."

"Aha! Therein lies the problem. I'm assuming you make the majority of your stops at various truck stops around the country?"

"Always."

"And those places are filled with clouds of smoke from the smoking drivers."

"Yes, it's definitely hard to breathe at times."

"Mr. Warner, I strongly suggest that you seek another line of employment for your physical well-being. Secondhand smoke is actually more damaging to your lungs than if you yourself were still smoking. Think about it, you are inhaling the most potent chemicals that have been exhaled by the smokers."

Richard took the advice of Dr. Stephen E. Possick to heart. In 1996, he was only sixty-one years old. He religiously kept his six-month checkups with Dr. Pradip Mishra in Clarksville, Tennessee. Dr. Mishra would routinely administer a dye solution that would enable him to diagnose the current status of Richard's heart. In 2005, Dr. Mishra discovered a problem with the mitral valve. He informed his patient of the seriousness of the situation and urged him to get the problem surgically repaired as soon as possible. He suggested that he contact Dr. Michael R. Petracek at nearby Vanderbilt Hospital in Nashville to perform the surgery. He further stated that Dr. Michael R. Petracek had successfully performed this delicate procedure fifty-three times.

Dr. Michael R. Petracek utilized robotic surgery in attaching a pig's vein to alleviate the problem.

"Straight from ole Charlie pig," the doctor mused.

Recovery was painful for the first month because of the incision marks caused by the robot that had penetrated through muscle tissue.

Family and friends would often inquire as to his physical status following his serious surgery. On one such occasion, whether from frustration or enlightenment, he blurted out, "I may smell like bacon, but I haven't oinked yet!"

2

PIERCED EARDRUMS

In 1938, two-year-old baby Richard A. Warner was having problems. For several weeks, the little baby had been in a fussing, distraught mood. He wasn't eating well, and his little hands kept pawing at his ears. Different prescribed medications didn't seem to help. Nighttime proved to be the most difficult for him. This is when the crying and screaming were the most pronounced. The only thing that seemed to alleviate the pain somewhat was when he was being held upright in a burping position. Friends and family members suggested that he must be a colic baby. He appeared to have many of the symptoms associated with a colic child. But Richard's mother didn't think so. She was sure that a colic baby exhibited these problems shortly after birth.

The Warner family lived in a modest home at 1405 Emerson Street, Northwest in Washington, DC. In this quiet neighborhood, they were blessed that their family doctor, Dr. David Davidson, made house calls. So before Mrs. Warner reached the pulling-out-hair stage, she summoned Dr. Davidson to the house. Dr. Davidson arrived early the next evening with his black satchel in hand.

"Well, you don't have to show me where the baby is—I can hear him!"

While Mrs. Warner held her screaming son firmly on her lap, Doc proceeded to carefully examine him. "His throat is beet red from all of the screaming. I can tell you his tonsils and adenoids are inflamed and will need to come out as soon as we clear this problem up. I need to take a close look at his ears now."

Doc intended to hold the ear carefully but firmly as he tried to peer inside the ear canal with the aid of a penlight. However, little Richard would have nothing to do with it as he thrashed about in pain.

"We need your husband to help us hold him still," Doc stated.

"Harold, we need your help in here, now!" Mrs. Warner pleaded.

Dr. Warner told the other two children to continue with their homework and hurried into the baby's room.

"What do you want me to do?" he asked.

"Could you help steady your son's head while I complete my inspection of his ears?"

Harold placed a large hand on each side of the baby's head.

"Thank you for your help! Your son has serious infection in each of his ear canals. We need to relieve the pressure that his eardrums are exerting."

"Are we going to have to take him to the hospital?" Mrs. Warner demanded.

"No, I need to start relieving some of the pressure right away."

"How are you going to do that, Doc?" Cynthia Warner cried out.

"I have some piercing needles in my case designed for this problem. As you know, these terrible earache incidents have been prevalent this winter amongst our younger children. Now if you will hold your son's head firmly in your hands, I'm going to attempt to pierce each eardrum a couple of times to relieve some of the intense pressure he is feeling."

After the first piercing, Richard's struggling and screaming intensified. It took several minutes of concerted efforts from everyone to finally achieve the necessary piercings. "We have some success," Doc exclaimed. "We now have some infected matter oozing out. This should help ease the pressure and pain somewhat for the poor lad."

Finally, Richard's sobbing and screaming subsided to a controllable whimper. Doc was then able to carefully removethe infectious material with some cotton swabs. He then handed Cynthia a small bottle of medicated eardrops and informed her to use the attached dropper to place a drop in each ear morning and night.

"I'm afraid we're going to have to follow this procedure a few more times in order to clear it up. As I mentioned to you earlier, once we have safely solved this problem, we need to have his tonsils and adenoids removed. They have greatly contributed to his ear situations. I will see you again in two days."

Doc arrived promptly two days later for his second appointment. Cynthia related that baby Richard had a restless first day following the initial piercings and the screaming had been minimal. However, the discomfort level had returned. Doc had Cynthia and Harold secure baby Richard in their arms and hands as he attempted four more piercings. As soon as had pierced the baby's right eardrum, the baby went into uncontrollable hysterics.

"We're going to have to come up with another solution to secure the baby. If we don't, I'm afraid I might make a mistake."

"What do you suggest we do, Doc?" Harold asked.

While Doc and Harold discussed what to try in order to rectify the problem, Cynthia had placed a baby blanket around baby Richard as he continued to sob.

"That's it!" Doc enthused.

"Huh?" Harold asked.

"We need to firmly wrap the baby in a blanket with his arms at his sides. Then our only problem will be keeping his head still. And I believe you can do that, Harold."

This solution did work, and it took a total of five house calls and eighteen piercings to achieve the desired outcome. Six months after the terrible earaches had cleared up, baby Richard's tonsils and adenoids were surgically removed.

The normal behavior of a vibrant two-year-old boy was a welcome relief to the Warner household.

3

HIDE-A-BED

During the WWII era, Richard's mom utilized their three-story Victorian house as a small (10 students) private boarding school for visiting foreign diplomatic families in Washington, DC. Over the ensuing years, the popularity and reputation of the small private school grew, and with the student enrollment reaching 125 students, Cynthia Warner decided to sell her private school.

In the beginning of this educational endeavor, the staff consisted of the following individuals:

- Mrs. Warner was principal and teacher of all disciplines at all levels.
- Richard's grandmother was responsible for home economics.
- A widow, Mrs. Helen Sully, taught math and science.

In 1947, Richard's uncle, J. Allen Crocker, who had returned from Los Alamos, New Mexico, where he had been instrumental in the development of the atomic bomb, was employed by Mrs. Warner to convert a small building located behind the house into a kindergarten classroom. This small building had been used as a catch-all storage facility. Mr. Crocker's renovated classroom featured a cupola with a school bell in it.

One evening when bed time was approaching, four-year-old Richard received a rude awakening. Mrs. Warner who sported long, well-manicured fingernails would pinch his earlobe between her forefinger and thumb when she wanted his immediate attention.

"You come with me young man," she admonished him.

"I didn't do nothing wrong," he whined.

"It's *anything wrong*," she retorted. She half dragged him into the living room area on the second floor, which was used for one of the classrooms. "Now help me move the desks to each side of the room so we can make room for a fold-out hide-a-bed."

"What's a fold hide-a-thingy?" the young lad inquired.

"It's a bed that folds up like this." She demonstrated by raising her arms from her sides above her head.

"Oh, okay," he murmured, still somewhat confused.

After the few desks were moved, she rolled the hide-a-bed out from a nearby closet. "Watch out," she warned Richard as she unfolded the bed. "Now you stay here by the bed while I get some bedding and a pillow."

Once the hide-a-bed was made up in sleeping condition, Mrs. Warner sat on the edge of the bed and sat her young son on her lap. "Do you know why I'm placing the hide-a-bed here in the middle of the classroom?" she asked him.

"Well, maybe because someone has to sleep on it," he replied.

"You're right, she said, "and do you know who that someone might be?"

"A new boarder," he stated.

"No, it's going to be you."

"Why?"

"Because, I can't have you sleeping in one of the bedrooms with someone else."

"Why not?"

"The number one problem is that you are still wetting in the bed. And number two, your urine stinks and I've been getting complaints."

"But I don't want to be by myself. I might get scared!"

"Well, that's just the way it's going to be, young man. When you quit wetting the bed, you will get your own bed and be able to move back into a bedroom."

The daily procedure of setting up the hide-a-bed after classes and then folding it up, storing it in the closet, and placing the desks back in rows continued for the next two years. Finally, at the age of six, Richard's bed wetting came to a halt.

True to her word, Mrs. Warner rewarded Richard with a new bed made out of maple, and he was given his own bedroom.

4

FAMILY PETS

Family pets, most noticeably dogs, became the prominent thing to invest in for family members in the 1940s and the 1950s. Thanks to radio and television, youngsters all over the country wanted a puppy.

During World War II, Fala, FDR's black Scottish terrier, become the darling of the political establishment. Chips, a mixture of German shepherd, collie, and husky, was the most decorated dog in World War II. And Judy, a pointer, was the only dog in the war to be registered as a prisoner of war.

The tragic hero of the 1950s movies was Old Yeller, a mixed Labrador retriever dog, and the darling of the television screen was Rin Tin Tin, a male German shepherd dog.

The Warner family was no exception. They loved their pets. Richard could recall at age four they had a black pedigreed cocker spaniel named Sooty. Everyone loved Sooty. He had long ears that drooped to the floor, and he was very playful. To get your attention, he would look up at you with those sad, droopy eyes of his. At age four, Richard often felt that his mother loved the dog more than she loved him. Of course, in all reality the dog was less maintenance.

The large Victorian house that the Warner family owned was also used as a private boarding school for foreign diplomatic families. Mrs. Warner had a firm belief in a well-rounded education for her students. As such, she provided them with a menagerie of animals, birds, and fish. Their very spacious living room showcased a large aquarium with a variety of fish. Many of the students enjoyed reading quietly near the aquarium with the soothing rhythm of the water permeating the air. Of the various types of birds they had the most popular were two singing yellow canaries.

When Richard was eight years old, the family purchased a sheep, aptly called Lamby. If he was being ignored, Lamby would give you a good butt to get your attention. Richard and some of his classmates loved to tease Richard's father. On a summer day in the late afternoon, Dr. Warner loved to recline in the large hammock situated on the veranda in the front of the house. They would place Lamby on the veranda and coax him in the direction of Mr. Warner. As if on cue, Lamby would rush to the hammock looking for some attention from Dr. Warner, and not receiving immediate attention, he would start head butting the hammock, which not only startled Dr. Warner, but elicited from him a few choice expletives.

One Easter, Dr. Warner had purchased three ducks for everyone to enjoy playing with. It didn't take but a matter of a few days for the quacking ducks to get on the adults' nerves, so the decision was made to load them up in the station wagon and haul them to Rock Creek Park and set them free. But every attempt to encourage them to stay at the park failed; they just keep waddling back to the car. After returning to the house, a spacious chicken wire fence was constructed away from the house to keep the ducks in.

During these formative school years, Richard would gather several box turtles that would occasionally wander onto their spacious yard. He kept them in a couple of large cardboard boxes. The students loved playing with them, and Richard taught them how to feed them with appropriate amounts of lettuce and carrots. And for a short amount of time, Richard also had a hamster he enjoyed playing with.

The last dog Richard could recall the family having was a pedigreed Irish setter named Rusty. Rusty was his brother Robert's (Bobby) dog. Rusty was a beloved dog who would nudge your hand when he wanted to be petted. Alas, Rusty would succumb to a rat's bite.

Unfortunately, after Richard joined the navy and he and Druwanda were married, pets were taboo in their household. A scary experience with a dog her family once had most probably influenced her disdain for animals. As a consequence, her children were never exposed to pets until Daree entered high school. Most probably she was influenced by her friends, and as a consequence, she sweet-talked Richard into getting her a pedigreed cocker spaniel whom she fondly called Dandy. However, Dandy thought he was a rottweiler and was constantly attacking people. In addition, he had a nasty habit of eating his own excrement. The Warners and the dog soon parted company.

It would be some thirty-eight to forty years later before Richard would have contact with a house pet. And this time it would be a tabby cat named Mietze I owned by Erica. This cat was a hunter, and it would often bring a dead mouse or, on occasion, a dead chipmunk and place it on the front porch.

Mietze I was followed some years later by Mietze II, who was a calico cat. This feline is definitely a house cat who loves to curl up on your lap.

5

CHRISTMAS AT THE WARNER HOUSEHOLD, CIRCA 1940S

Following Thanksgiving, the weeks leading up to Christmas 1940 in the Warner household were an exciting and frustrating time for four-year-old Richard. The excitement was twofold for him: trying to help out with the family's busy preparations during the Christmas season with their ten-foot Christmas tree being the main focal point and fuming and fussing over what to expect from Santa Claus.

The tree of choice was a tall Scotch pine. Richard's two older brothers, William (Billy) and Robert (Bobby), were assigned to get the tree from a neighbor's pasture that was dotted with a variety of several trees. Dr. Warner gave his sons specific instructions regarding the tree they were to select for display in their spacious living room. The tree needed to be nearly ten feet tall and symmetrical. If the tree was over ten feet tall, they would saw the necessary inches off from the base of the tree. The ceilings in the Warner household were ten feet tall, and Mr. Warner insisted that the tree almost reach the ceiling. Enough room was saved for the angel that would adorn the top of the tree.

Billy and Bobby would head out to their neighbor's property with the family's horses, Bessie and Bonnie, to fetch the Christmas tree. Dr. Warner had purchased the horses from the army for a few dollars, and they were used primarily for riding purposes and to help with some designated chores. Richard's brothers took along a bucksaw to cut down the tree and a rope harness to drag the tree home. Once they had cut down the selected tree, they would secure the rope harness to the trunk of the tree and then slowly and carefully drag the tree home attached to the two horses.

Once the Scotch pine was firmly secured in its tree stand, the decoration of the tree began. This was exciting for Richard as it was a family project. The first order of business was to place the angel on the top of the tree. It didn't take much coaxing from Richard's dad to get him excited to be the chosen one to place the angel on the top of the tree. Dr. Warner secured Richard tightly to his side with his left arm as he ascended the ladder. Richard was clutching the angel in his tiny fists when his dad stopped a few feet from the top of the ladder. He carefully hoisted the boy with his two hands a few inches from the apex of the tree. After a few tries, Richard succeeded in placing the angel on the tree.

Before the actual decorating of the tree began in earnest, Mrs. Warner placed a fluffy cotton material under the Christmas tree to give an aura of snow under it. The tree then cast a shimmering glow from the silver tinsel that was profusely hung from it. Billy and Bobby helped their father haul up ten boxes of Christmas bulbs to be hung strategically on branches of the tree. Little Richard began whining, "Me wanna do it!"

His mother was quick to admonish him, "Richard, it's *I want to do it!*"

"I wanna do it!" he responded.

"Here, you can try one." His dad chuckled as he handed him a bulb.

Richard waddled to the tree, and to his dismay he dropped the bulb, which shattered all over the floor.

"That's enough, young man," his mom proclaimed as she pinched his earlobe.

By the time Christmas actually rolled around, the boys had the toy section of the Montgomery Wards catalog practically torn to shreds. They had to submit a list of not more than three items they would like to have. Of course, they were cautioned that any presents from Santa Claus was predicated on their good behavior. What made the passage of time more unbearable was for them having to stare at the Christmas stockings with their names on them arrayed on the

22

mantel of the fireplace. However, being able to set and watch the Lionel train chug around the tracks under the Christmas tree helped the time go by. And listening to some of the popular Christmas songs on their Motorola radio definitely kept them in the mood. Songs such as "White Christmas," "Jingle Bells," and "Rudolph the Red Nosed Reindeer" were among their favorites. The choir at their church would sometimes sing "Silent Night" in German, which Richard's parents enjoyed hearing:

> Stille Nacht
> Stille Nacht! Heil'ge Nacht!
> Alles schlaff; einsam wacht
> Nur das traute hoch heilige Paar.
> Holder Knab' im lockigen Haar,
> Schafe in himmlischar Ruh!

When Christmas Eve came and they were finally handed their Christmas stockings, they discovered a Christmas card on top addressed especially to each of them. The bulk of the stocking consisted of candy canes and an assortment of fruit. Tucked away in the toe of the stocking was a silver dollar from Santa!

Ironically during those early Christmas years, Richard treasured those items that he received that had his initials, RAW, on them because he didn't have to share them with his siblings. A couple of the memorable items he received were a pair of velvet trousers with a maroon stripe down the pant legs and a clothes brush that was decorated in gold leaf.

In 1946, when Richard was ten years old, he was really looking forward to the coming Christmas season. It was finally his turn to get to help cut down the Christmas tree! He enjoyed working the bucksaw with his brother Bobby to fell that perfect Scotch pine. Shortly afterward. Richard became very sick with a high fever and swelling of the glands in his throat area. It didn't take long for him to become disoriented and to have trouble with his breathing. Becoming increasingly alarmed, Mrs. Warner rushed Richard to the hospital, where he was diagnosed with erysipelas—an acute bacterial disease marked by fever and severe skin inflammation.

Several different medications were administered, but to no avail. The medical staff reluctantly informed Mrs. Warner that her son was probably going to die. She blurted out, "No way! My son is going to live! Try that new drug that just came out called penicillin!"

They consented to give it a try. The results were miraculous! Richard was soon able to return home. It was definitely a Christmas he would always remember!

6

THE LOOK

Most every family in Richard's neighborhood in the 1930s and 1940s had their own strict discipline measures that they enforced, and Richard's family was no exception.

Mrs. Warner's most effective and feared method of discipline she employed with her boarding students and her family members was when she used her long, sharp fingernail to pinch the earlobe of the offending culprit. She would then lead the guilty offender to the privacy of her office for a verbal reprimand that was appropriate for the crime.

Interestingly enough, no one could ever recall anyone's ear ever bleeding from this form of discipline. Mrs. Warner apparently had the pressure point technique of this method down to a science.

Even though Richard detested the times he was the recipient of such disciplinary measures, he remembered the time on a rather hot, muggy day in early September when his mother felt it necessary to lead him by pinched ear to the basement.

Richard was apparently ignoring the verbal warnings in Mrs. Helen Sully's science class. He continued to tease mercilessly a shy girl in the class with some earthworms they were supposed to be working with. Unfortunately for the lad, his mother had just stopped by to monitor the progress of the class. Once she heard Helen's irritated warning, she quickly had Richard by the ear and was escorting him from the classroom, much to the delight of the teacher and the other students.

She led her son down the steps of the basement. "Richard, this classroom behavior of yours has to stop *now*!

"Yes, ma'am," he muttered.

"This is the third time this week that you have failed to heed the warnings of your teachers, and you are frightening that shy little girl!"

"Yes, ma'am, I won't do it again!"

"Those are just your excuse words! But apparently, you need a firmer reminder of what *respect* actually means! 'Yes, ma'am, I won't do it again' appears to be just words on your part!"

Mrs. Warner grabbed the razor strop from the basement wall and instructed him to bend over the orange crate that was nearby on the floor.

"Please, Mom, I promise I won't do it again!" he pleaded.

"That's the purpose of this whipping," she affirmed in an elevated voice.

Four or five swats later, he was led by the ear, sobbing, back to the classroom. The visual effect registered on the students' faces was an added bonus to the discipline code.

However, Richard would always remember a hard lesson regarding respect for his mother which was paramount in the Warner household. Having endured several verbal warnings one particular day in the classroom and from his mother, Richard was not in an amicable mood during the family's evening meal. He ignored inquiries to how his classes were going, especially those coming from his mother.

"I understand you had some problems in math class today," his mother asked.

His reply was to give her a hard stare. Additional questions from her resulted in the same stare.

His dad had finally had enough of this disrespectful behavior from his son. He jumped up from his chair, grabbed Richard by the arm, and jerked him out of his chair. "How dare you give your mother *the look*!" he fumed.

"But, but, I—"

"No ifs, ands, or buts, young man! You're going to the basement with me!" He half dragged the young boy down the basement steps.

Once on the floor, with Richard still firmly in his grasp, he unbuckled his belt from his trousers and jerked it free.

"I don't ever want to see you *look* at your mother like that again!" With his son still firmly in his grip, he began to whip the boy on the back of his legs. He didn't let up with the lashings until his arm finally tired. "Now get up the stairs and apologize to your mother and then get to bed!" he shouted.

Shaking, and with bleeding legs, Richard fought back the tears as he painfully made his way up the stairs.

He would never *look* at his mother the same way again.

7

CAMP WACHUSETT, HERE I COME!

Richard was foaming at the bit. There was still a week left in the school term, and the excitement of getting to attend his first summer camp at Camp Wachusett in New Hampshire was becoming unbearable.

"I'm never going to get to go camp," Richard whined incessantly.

"Not if you keep that up, you are not," Mrs. Warner warned. "Just focus on your last week of school and getting your chores done, and it will be here before you know it."

Well, the much-anticipated moment had finally arrived. "Have you double-checked your suitcase to make sure all of your clothing and toiletry items have been properly packed?" Richard's mom asked.

"Yes, yes, I did! I marked each item off the list you gave me. Now can we go, please?"

"Your father had an administrator's meeting at his school, so I've arranged for a taxi to take you and Ms. Marion Hanawalt to the train station. She will chaperone you to the camp. Go ahead out to the front porch. The taxi will be here any minute now. Give me a hug, behave yourself, and remember your manners."

"Yes, ma'am." And with a quick wave of his hand, he hurried out of the house.

After Richard and Mrs. Hanawalt were situated in the back seat of the taxi, she cautioned him to stay close to her so they wouldn't get separated. "It's easy to get lost at the train station, and there are some unscrupulous characters lurking about. Do you understand me?" She said.

"Yes, Mrs. Hanawalt, I most surely do," he replied as he stared out the window at the passing scenery.

The taxi arrived at the B & O train station thirty minutes prior to their departure time. Marion paid the taxi driver, and he retrieved Richard's suitcase for him. They thanked him for safely delivering them to the train station and then made their way to the train terminal.

Marion picked up their train tickets at the ticket counter and, grabbing Richard firmly by the hand, led the gawking lad out to the spacious platform to await the arrival of their train. Finding a visible spot near a lamppost, Marion informed Richard that he needed to stay in the designated spot she pointed out to him. "I have to attend to some personal business, and I'll be right back," she informed him.

"Okay," he said. After a few minutes of fidgeting around, he moved some twenty feet from his "designated spot" so he could get a better view of the incoming trains. As he stared down the track, he felt a hand lightly on his shoulder. Half startled he turned to face a stranger.

"I didn't mean to scare you, boy," the pleasant-sounding man said.

"Wha…what do you want?" he stammered.

Pulling a bag of candy sweets from his shirt pocket, the stranger tempted Richard with it while dangling it in front of his face. "Come with me and it's all yours, boy," he urged.

"No!" Richard blurted out as he backed away from the stranger.

About that time, Mrs. Hanawalt appeared.

"Richard, what are you doing away from your spot?" she demanded.

The stranger quickly disappeared into the shadows.

"I just wanted to see when the train was coming."

"Well, the next time, you better heed what I tell you!"

In a few minutes, they boarded the train, and without further incident, they arrived in the small town of Holderness, where Camp Wachusett was located. After disembarking from the train, Mrs. Hanawalt reminded Richard to remember his mother's instructions, and then she bade him farewell. The young lad and a half dozen other campers who had been on the train only had to wait a few minutes before their ride to the camp arrived.

A flatbed Ford truck with protective railings on the sides, filled with a half dozen benches for the campers to sit on, was the makeshift mode of transportation used. The bumpy ride to the campsite only took ten to fifteen minutes as it was only a mile and a half away. Once they hopped down from the back of the truck and secured their luggage, the campers were escorted to their respective cabins. They deposited their luggage near their assigned bunks and were told to assemble in the quad area in front of the cabins.

Charlie, the head counselor, motioned for the campers to gather in a semicircle in front of him. Once the stragglers were in place, he stepped atop a small platform and asked for quiet.

Camp Wachusett main lodge

"Welcome to Camp Wachusett, boys! In a few minutes, I will dismiss you for lunch. Our lunchroom and recreational area for playing ping-pong, cards, and board games, etc., is located in the building in the center of the cabins. The latrine is located at the edge of the wooded area north of the cabins. Once you are finished with lunch, you may use the latrine if need be and then return to your designated cabins. At that time, you are to make up your bunk bed with the linen already placed on it. Your cabin counselor will aid you with this task. After you have placed the contents of your suitcase on the shelving in your bunk area, you are free to relax and get acquainted with your fellow campers. We will grill hot dogs out here in the quad area for dinner tonight. Chips and an array of fruit will also be served. When the meal is finished, we will try and answer any questions you may have. Before I let you go to lunch, I need to cover Camp Wachusett's rules with you. Here are your rules:

1. Follow all instructions given to you by your counselors.
2. Report all injuries and/or illnesses immediately to us.
3. Work in your assigned team areas.
4. Be a team player and do not venture away from camp by yourself.
5. No fighting with each other or disrespecting any of the camp counselors, and
6. Maintain proper hygiene practices.

"Remember, any violation of the above rules will result in appropriate punishments to be administered first thing in the mornings. Also, daily activities will be posted on the cabin doors each morning. First thing on the agenda tomorrow will be swimming practice in the roped-off area at the edge of the lake. You are dismissed. Have a great day!"

The evening cookout was followed by everyone stating their names and where they were from. A question-and-answer session ensued. The number one concern for the newly arrived campers was, "Are there any wild animals here?"

"To be truthful," Charlie replied, "although we rarely see any wild animals, a few have been reported from time to time. You may hear the cry of a wolf in the distance at night, and a bear has supposedly been seen a time or two. The point is, keep your distance and stay close to others, and you will be fine."

On that first night at camp as Richard lay in bed, he was having a meltdown. He had to go to the latrine, but he was terribly frightened. It was dark, the latrine was at the edge of the woods, and there might be a bear lurking nearby. He was afraid to awaken any of the other campers or the counselor. Richard hadn't wet the bed in over four years, so he was praying this time he could withstand the mounting pressure.

At six the next morning, the camp counselor urged everyone to rise and get dressed as quickly as possible. Charlie was ordering everyone to meet in the quad area ASAP.

A confused bunch of half-awake campers gathered at the quad. After all campers were accounted for, Charlie raised his arms for silence. In an elevated voice, he began his rant. "We've had a violation of one of our rules, boys, and this is just our first night here! It seems rule number 6 regarding personal hygiene has been broken. Camp Wachusett's motto has always been, 'One for all, all for one.' In this case, one violation results in the punishment of all. Apparently one of our cabin counselors discovered early this morning on his routine bed check that one of the campers had wet his bed—big time! So all must be punished, wouldn't you agree, Mr. Warner?"

"No-o, I do-don't think I do-o—"

"Sorry, incorrect response! Here's the punishment. Every camper will line up single file behind Louie. The rest of you camp counselors will line up approximately three to five yards behind me and then follow my lead when we get started. We are going to spread our legs shoulder width apart and bend at the waist. We will be administering a whipping with the palm of our hands on your behinds. Louie, begin!"

One by one the campers crawled nervously between the counselors' legs. It appeared to Richard, who was halfway back in the line, that the campers were only receiving one token hand slap on their rear ends. This wasn't going to be as bad as he thought.

When his turn came, he dropped to his knees and began his crawl.

"Well, well," Charlie stated, "if it isn't Camper Warner, who thought the punishment shouldn't be for all!"

With that utterance, he gave Richard as many hand slaps as could muster, and the rest of the counselors followed suit. Richard bit his tongue to keep from yelling in pain. He emerged from the ordeal red faced, grabbing his behind.

It was obvious to the other campers who followed Richard through the gauntlet and to the ones who had preceded him who the guilty party was. They ignored him for a couple of days, but soon let him back into the fold, as one of his fellow campers remembered that Richard had denied that all of them should be punished.

The rest of the camp went by quickly and without incident. Richard's folks picked him up in their station wagon at the end of the fun-filled camp, and the family then spent the next week at a rented cabin near Palmer Lake. During their stay at the cabin, Richard's mom often quizzed him about the activities he and the other campers at Camp Wajusik were engaged in. One evening, she changed tactics in her questioning. She asked him point-blank if he had been disciplined for any infraction of the camp rules or the initial instructions she had given him prior to camp.

With a pensive look on his face, Richard shrugged his shoulders and meekly replied, "Not that I can think of, Mom."

8

ONE HALF OF THE PEACE SIGN—ALMOST!

At age 12, Richard was promoted to mowing the lawn. The family's three-story Victorian home was situated on 2.57 acres of land. So with the old push lawnmower, it was a daunting task to mow. In May 1948, Richard's folks purchased a relatively new Craftsman power lawnmower from Richard's uncle, J. Allen Crocker. He had purchased the lawnmower from Sears & Roebuck, and it was powered by a Briggs & Stratton four-cycle engine. The engine turned a shaft that was equipped with two belt pulleys. These belts from the main engine shaft ran to the pulleys on the drive shaft located on the inside of each of the wheels on the outside of the mower. This was a prototype of the self-propelled lawnmowers that would become popular years later.

With this new machine to work with, Richard was in hog heaven. He couldn't wait to get started. In his excited state, he forgot his mother's number 1 instruction he needed to do before mowing. He was supposed to scan the entire area looking for obstacles that would interfere with his mowing, such as rocks, trash, or toys.

After three pulls on the starter rope, the Briggs & Stratton engine roared to life. Richard made two swaths around the perimeter of the lawn and decided to mow back and forth in a vertical pattern. Several swaths later in the middle of the lawn, the lawnmower came to an abrupt halt. A loud clanking noise rudely startled Richard as he was thrust into the mower's handlebars.

Once he got over the initial shock of what had just happened, Richard began to assess the damage and the cause of the mower's malfunction. As he examined the front of the mower, he discovered a metal toy shovel jammed in the mower's blades. After much tugging and yanking, he was able to dislodge the damaged toy. Careful visual inspection revealed what appeared to be just a slight alteration to a couple of the blades.

Feeling somewhat relieved, he attempted to start the engine again. The out-of-alignment of the mower blades caused them to make a clanking noise as Richard tried to move the mower forward. The belts on the outside wheel pulleys seemed stuck somehow. He attempted to eliminate the problem by trying to pull the belt forward on the right wheel pulley. He yanked on the belt near the backside of the top of the pulley.

When the power from the engine and Richard's tugging on the belt caught hold, his middle finger on his right hand between the front and middle knuckle was almost severed as it was jerked under the belt around the pulley. He was in a state of shock as he looked at his fingertip, which was dangling by a sliver of skin and tissue and spurting blood everywhere.

Once the realization of what had happened had sunk in, Richard cradled his injured hand in the palm of his left hand and went screaming bloody murder into the house.

His mother hastened from the kitchen into the front foyer of the house. "Calm down, Richard, what happened?"

"I got my finger caught in the mower," he sobbed as he revealed his finger to her.

"Oh my God!" she exclaimed. She quickly ushered him into the kitchen and wrapped a small cloth around his injured hand. "Hold this carefully in your other hand," she cautioned as she hustled him out of the house.

After getting Richard situated in the passenger seat of the car, Mrs. Warner hopped into the driver's seat. The half-mile drive to the doctor's office took just seconds to navigate. She came to a screeching halt and rushed him inside.

On examining Richard's almost severed finger, Dr. Brownsberger, their family doctor, said, "I'm afraid we need to amputate the boy's finger."

"What?" Richard's mother exclaimed. "No way are you going to cut off my boy's finger. You are going to reattach it!"

"But, Mrs. Warner, we really need to amputate!"

"You are going to sew the tip of his finger back on! Now!" she warned him.

"Okay, okay," he conceded. "Nurse, call Doctors Jurgen and Hopper to assist me and prepare the young man for surgery."

"Yes, Doctor, right away!" she replied.

In a matter of minutes, everything was ready. "Mrs. Warner, I want you wait here while we attempt to reattach the boy's finger. It might take a number of hours to accomplish. I've never attempted this before."

"No way, Doctor, I will be in there with my boy!" she demanded.

"Okay, but you must wear a mask and gown the nurse will give you."

Only a localized pain sedative was available and as the doctors worked feverishly to attempt the delicate task of reattaching the fingertip, Richard was screaming at the top of his lungs in excruciating pain. After listening to her son's agony for several minutes, Mrs. Warner stepped in by her son's side and stated, "Doctors, please excuse me for a moment."

She gripped her son firmly on his shoulder, stared at him face-to-face, and warned him, "If you don't stop crying, I'm going to give you something to cry about!"

Richard's crying and screaming subsided to a low whimpering noise.

Richard was dismissed following surgery with his right arm in a makeshift sling. For his sixth-grade graduation, his mother made him a new arm sling out of some navy blue and gold material, which was the private school's colors.

One morning a few weeks after school was out in June, Mrs. Warner noticed at the breakfast table that there were some notice-

I MAY SMELL LIKE BACON BUT I HAVEN'T OINKED YET

able purple streaks crawling up Richard's right arm. She immediately rushed him back to the doctor's office.

"This is terrible," Dr. Brownsberger said. "I was afraid this might happen. We're going to need to amputate the boy's arm!"

"Oh, no, you're not!" Mrs. Warner insisted. "You're going to give him some of that new drug called penicillin to clear this up!"

"Well, let's see, that new experimental drug has shown great promise."

"Can you get some?" she inquired.

"I think so."

"Then let's try it," she enthused.

Within a day after the penicillin shot had been administered, a big improvement could be detected. And in a matter of a few weeks, the problem was totally cleared up.

Richard learned a valuable lesson from this painful ordeal: never underestimate the power of your mother.

Photo Credit, Paul K. Williams 11/1999—
Courtesy of the Maryland Historic Trust

9

WESTWARD, HO!

At age 15, Richard was elated! His brother Robert, who was attending vet school at Iowa State College in Ames, Iowa, invited him to spend the summer with him and his wife, Carol. He boarded the B & O railroad passenger train late one afternoon in early June. The anxiety of the long train journey to Ames, Iowa, was made most memorable by the late-night ride through Pittsburgh, Pennsylvania. The night sky was brilliantly ablaze from the fire furnaces of the massive steel mills. Richard secretly wondered if this was what hell looked like. He was glad he was safely secured in the train compartment.

Richard's brother Robert and his wife, Carol, picked him from the train station early the following morning. After helping him get settled in their small apartment located near the college, they gave him a tour of the campus area. Robert informed him what building he was to report to in order to begin his summer job. Carol said she would introduce him to his boss as she was a lab assistant in the same building.

The next morning, following a hurried breakfast of bacon, eggs, and toast, Carol escorted Richard to the college genetics lab building and introduced him to his boss, Professor Smithberg. The professor informed him that his job, although a simple one, would command his attention to detail. He was to keep the lab animal cages cleaned and sterilized.

"One of my lab assistants, Joe, will teach you the proper techniques in accomplishing these cleaning tasks. He will show you where the cleaning supplies are kept, and how to properly clean the cages, and where to safely dispose of the cleanings. Any questions, young man?"

"No, sir!"

"Good, you will assist Joe for the next week, and then you will be on your own."

Richard was a quick study and soon had his work detail down pat. In fact, Professor Smithberg was impressed with his efficiency in accomplishing his tasks. He was compensated with a salary of $19 a month.

On weekends Richard would often accompany Robert to the local dump, where they would scavenge for usable lumber. His brother was very adept at making necessary furniture for the apartment. One of the projects was a shower rack that could be used for shower items and as a foot stool.

Richard was assigned household chores to do, including helping with meal preparations. Chicken was one of the main staples of their meals. They were on a tight budget, and chicken was relatively cheap. Robert and Carol were very creative with their chicken dinners.

Robert would buy a crate of live six to eight chickens at a local farmers' market. Richard's task was to chop off the chickens' heads and then take them into the kitchen, where his brother had a pot of hot water ready. Richard was instructed to grab the chicken by both of its legs, lay it face down on the railroad tie that was located in the back of the apartment, and then chop its head off with the hatchet. He grabbed a chicken out of the crate, held its legs firmly in his left hand, and placed it face up on the railroad tie. With a quick whack of the hatchet, he severed the chicken's head. The instinctive response from the chicken was a furious flapping of its wings, which caused the blood spurting neck to splatter Richard with a crimson bath of red spots. After the initial shock of the unexpected was over, he took the chicken into the apartment's kitchen, where his brother was waiting.

"My God, what happened to you?" Robert asked as he burst into laughter.

"It's not funny!" Richard muttered.

"Well, you were so excited to help me, you didn't listen carefully enough to my instructions. Hold the chicken's facedown before you chop its head off and you won't have to deal with its flapping wings."

Preparing the rest of the chickens for the boiling pot went smoothly, without any further problems.

A real treat one evening was when Robert and Carol took Richard to Boone, Iowa, for a Dairy Queen treat. The twenty-five-cent ice cream cone was the best he had ever tasted.

All too soon, the end of summer was at hand. Robert informed his younger brother that he would be taking him to the train station at the end of the week for his return trip back east.

It was hard saying goodbye to Robert for two reasons; he thoroughly enjoyed bonding with his brother, and he knew he would miss the freedom of being his own man. Once he got his luggage secured, he looked for a comfortable seat in the passenger car. When he ambled down the aisle, he spotted a beautiful young lady who was sitting by herself. As he approached, she glanced up and gave him an approving smile. Gathering up his courage, he timidly asked if the vacant seat across from her was taken.

"Why, no!" she enthused.

They proceeded to awkwardly introduce themselves to each other. Her name was Mary Bradford, and she attended a private school much like the one his mother ran. They eagerly exchanged stories of their families, friends, and school. Before they knew it, the sun was setting as they were entering into the Pittsburg area. They both marveled at the brilliant fiery glow emanating from the steel mill furnaces.

Richard was totally smitten by this fair maiden—he was in love! Before they realized it, they were fast approaching their destination. He bravely asked Mary for her address so that he might write to her. She was happy to comply and handed him a folded slip of paper with her name and address on it.

He held the precious note in his left hand with his train ticket and carried his luggage in his right hand. The train attendant grabbed the ticket from his hand, punched it, and placed it back in his hand.

When they left the passenger car, Mary spotted her parents to her left several feet down the waiting platform; likewise, Richard spied his folks to his right.

"Please write," Mary hollered as she headed for her family.

"I will!" Richard shouted.

On the drive home, Richard told his parents about all his experiences at his brother's place in Iowa, but he couldn't wait to get home so he could write a letter to the love of his life.

The few minutes it took to get home seemed like an eternity to Richard. As soon as he entered the house, he rushed upstairs to his room and tossed his luggage on the bed. He then began a frantic search for the lovely young lady's precious note. After turning every pocket inside out, to no avail, he sat totally dejected on the edge of his bed.

Apparently when he left the passenger car, the note had slipped from his hand when the train attendant was punching his ticket. Richard was so taken in by this beautiful young lady that he not only didn't have her address, he couldn't even remember her name!

10

AN APPLE A DAY

As Eve was tempted with an apple by the devil in the Garden of Eden, so too were Richard and his brother Robert (Bobby) tempted by the apples on the trees on the Warners' property. On the south side of their large Victorian house were five apple trees and one crab apple tree. Three of the trees produced Grimes apples, a variety of golden apples. And two produced the Red Delicious, which the boys fondly referred to as sheep noses, due to the shape of the bottom of the apples.

The crab apple tree, although a prolific producer of fruit, was taboo as the apples were extremely tart to the taste and very hard.

At ten years of age, Richard couldn't wait for the apples to ripen thoroughly. Once they exhibited a reddish or golden hue, he figured they were ready to eat. Early one autumn day, temptation got the better of him. He yanked one golden apple and one red delicious apple from the trees. Poking his head around the tree, he did a quick surveillance to see if anyone was watching him. Satisfied that he was alone, he hurried behind the house and headed for the south end of the family's garage, which sat several feet north of the house.

Out of breath from the run to the garage, he peered around both ends of it to see if he was still in the clear. Satisfied that he was definitely alone, he slumped down with his back to the wall. He carefully rubbed each apple on his shirt until they exhibited a shiny glow. Now he was ready to enjoy the fruits of his escapade. The first bite was from the Grimes golden apple, followed by a bite from the Red Delicious apple. Each apple had a distinctive taste that he savored.

The only problem he noticed was that both apples had a rather tough texture to them, so each bite required a prolonged chewing effort.

When he was finished eating the apples, he discarded the apple cores by tossing them in the neighbor's backyard. A few minutes later, he spotted his brother Bobby working in the garden on the south side of the house. On his way to the garden, he was distracted by some chattering birds in their big oak tree. He retreated quickly to the gravel driveway near the garage and scooped up a handful of rocks for ammunition. As he came within in firing range of the elm tree, he began hurling rock after rock into the branches of the tree. Several birds began scattering in all directions to avoid the incoming missiles, much to the delight of Richard.

"Hey, Richard, get over here and help me in the garden!" Bobby yelled.

"Huh, okay, I'm coming," Richard replied. "What do you need help with?"

"Grab that hoe near the gate and help me finishing weeding these rows. I want to get done before lunch is ready."

They finished just as their mother hollered out, "Lunchtime, boys!"

Suddenly Richard grabbed Bobby by his shoulder with one hand and clutched at his stomach with his other hand. "My stomach hurts!" he cried out.

"You're not getting the flu, are you?" Bobby inquired.

"I...I don...don't think so," he uttered.

Aided by his brother, they soon entered into the kitchen.

"Richard, what's the matter with you? You look peaked," his mother asked.

"I, I don't know. My stomach hurts bad!"

"What were you eating?" she demanded.

"Well, I, I ate some apples!"

"Richard, you know better! Those apples won't be ready to eat for another two weeks! Bobby, help him into the bathroom, I'll be there in a moment."

Mrs. Warner quickly dissolved some baking soda in a warm glass of water and joined her sons in the bathroom. "Here, Richard, drink this down, now!"

"But, but, Mom…"

"No buts! Do it now!" she warned him as she pinched his earlobe between her thumb and forefinger.

Grabbing the sides of the sink with his hands for support, Richard threw up. After a few more upchucks, he stood exhausted and shaking uncontrollably over the sink.

"Well, young man, do you think you have learned your lesson?"

"Ye-s, ye-s, Mom!"

Unfortunately, the same scenario occurred each of the next two years. However, the third time did prove to be the charm.

A problem arose as the apples fully ripened on the trees. Several of them were being invaded by fruit worms. Rather than discard them as they were instructed to do, Bobby had Richard help him pick the infected apples and put them in a basket. Bobby had inherited a "no throwaway" policy from his dad, who had suffered financially through the Great Depression.

"What are we going to do with these apples, Bobby? They're no good."

"Oh yes, they are! We're going to make some apple cider out of them."

"How are we going to do that?"

"Grab a handle on the basket and help me carry it to the house and I'll show you."

A table at one end of the large pantry room had a meat grinder attached to it. Bobby placed a large pan under the spout of the grinder. "Now I'm going to turn the crank, and you drop an apple in the top opening one at a time," Bobby instructed his brother.

"But what about the worms?"

"Oh, they're good for you. They're a good source of protein."

"I don't know about that!"

"You'll see. Trust me!"

After all the apples met their fate in the meat grinder, the large pan was brimming full with a delicious odor from the apple mash.

"Are we going to eat that?" Richard wanted to know.

"No, we've got another process to run through, and then we'll be able to drink it."

Bobby searched the pantry area until he found an empty, clean flour sack. As he held the flour sack open over the huge sink located near the table, he had Richard carefully dumped the apple mash from the pan into it. Once this was accomplished, he twisted the open end tightly shut. After he had Richard clean out the pan with warm water and dry it, he began squeezing the apple mash in the flour sack over the pan while Richard held the top of the sack firmly in his hands. Liquid apple cider soon began flowing out of the flour sack. Richard was amazed at how much liquid was in the pan. The next step was to thoroughly rinse out the flour sack, hang it out to dry, and get rid of the remnants of the apple mash.

The final step was to pour the cider into a glass container. While Bobby searched the pantry for an empty milk jar, Richard looked for a funnel they could use. Bobby then poured the apple cider into the funnel that Richard held firmly over the milk jar.

When they were finished, Bobby poured a small glassful for each of them to sample and placed the remainder in the refrigerator.

"To us!" Bobby declared as he toasted his younger brother.

Richard was surprised. It did taste good, although he still had doubts about the worms.

11

EAT, DRINK, AND BE MERRY!

"Bobby, make yourself and your brother Richard some lunch. I'm meeting with some parents in my office."

"Okay, Mom!"

Running a private school as owner, principal, and teacher kept Mrs. Warner very busy, and she depended on her sons to not only toe the line but also to help out when needed.

"What are we going to have?" Richard taunted his brother. "I'm hungry!"

"Let me see what I can find in the fridge," Bobby answered.

"Well, hurry up, I'm starving!"

"Bite your tongue and set the table. Get some bowls instead of plates out and a couple of spoons. All I see is a bunch of leftovers. Hey! I know what, I'll throw a bunch of it into a pot, and we'll have some homemade stew!"

"Ugh! Sounds terrible to me!" Richard grimaced.

"Be quiet and pour each of us a glass of water. This should only take a few minutes." Bobby then commenced to dump anything that looked edible into the pot, including various vegetables and meats. Some of the meats and veggies he had to chop up before putting them in the pot. After adding some water, he placed the lid on the pot and lit the stove burners. "Be ready in about five minutes," he said.

In a matter of minutes, the stew was ready, and Booby filled their bowls and fetched some saltine crackers from the pantry.

After tentatively tasting a spoonful, Richard announced, "Hey, this isn't too bad!"

Bobby gave him a satisfactory grin as he sampled his first spoonful. Growing up in challenging times often required a make-do attitude.

As a youngster, Richard wanted to emulate his father and his brother. Bobby had a unique talent that he was envious of. He would toss a kernel of popcorn or a peanut into the air and then catch it with his wide-open mouth.

"Let me try it, let me try it!" Richard pleaded.

"Well, the bowl of popcorn is there on the table. Grab a kernel and give it a try!"

Richard grabbed one and tossed it in the air—it didn't even hit his face. Several attempts later, the floor was littered with popcorn. His frustration was compounded by his brother poking fun at his failures.

A few days later, Richard was practicing catching some peanuts he was tossing into the air. After numerous futile misses, he stopped, shrugged off his disappointment, and focused. He carefully tossed a peanut straight up in the air and caught it in his mouth. He was concentrating so hard that his mouth was almost in a lockjaw position, which caused the peanut to lodge in his windpipe. He sputtered and coughed, trying to dislodge the peanut, to no avail. Fortunately, his mother was aware of his distressful situation.

She applied a few solid thumbs with the back of her hand to his upper back, but Richard was still thrashing about. She grabbed him firmly by the arm and quickly rushed him to the station wagon and sped to the nearest emergency facility a half mile away.

"What's the young man gotten himself into this time?" the doctor asked.

"Oh, he was playing around with his food and got a peanut lodged in his windpipe," Mrs. Warner said.

After a quick examination, the doctor determined that they would have to insert a suction tube down his throat to dislodge the peanut.

While Richard's mom held his head in her hands in a slightly backward position, the attending nurse held his mouth open and used a tongue depressor to hold his tongue in place. The doctor then inserted the suction tube and after a few tries was able to successfully remove the peanut.

On the short ride back home, Richard's mom admonished him, "You're just never going to learn, are you, boy!"

It was a different story with his dad. Richard envied the luxury that apparently only his dad could indulge in. The Great Depression and the rationing associated with the sacrifices demanded by World War II kept the family's food and drink purchases to necessary items only.

However, his dad was able to cope with these meager times by occasionally having a Pepsi Cola. Richard would watch his dad pop the cap off the bottle of cola and take a long swig from it. He asked several times for his dad to give him a drink, but the stern look from his father ended his pleas. Richard then began to silently stalk his dad when he drank his cola. Unfortunately, most of the time there was nothing left in the glass.

However, one evening as his dad was enjoying his cola, his mother entered the kitchen to inform him that a gentleman at the front door wished to converse with him. Dr. Warner got up from his chair and placed his glass near the sink and hurried out of the kitchen.

Richard waited carefully for a few minutes to make sure his dad wasn't returning. He rushed over to the sink and noticed that there was still some cola in the bottom of the glass. Glancing quickly from side to side, he grabbed the glass and devoured the cola.

"Wha-what?" Something seemed to be momentarily lodged in his throat. A quick gulp, and everything was clear. He soon spied a centipede behind the sink. He grabbed a napkin and squashed it and then tossed it in the trash can.

Oh my God, he thought, *I bet I just swallowed a centipede that must have fallen into the cola!*

Panic set in and he rushed into the bathroom grabbing at his throat. But his throat felt fine, and he didn't feel anything crawling around in his stomach. After he had settled down, he noticed a partially filled glass of water near the sink. In it was a dead moth. At this time of year the Miller moths were invading the area, so he figured he must have ingested one of them.

His dad's colas no longer intrigued him.

12

Sandlot Kickball

Most every young boy growing up in the city at one time or another played a version of some sandlot sport. Stick baseball was probably the most popular, followed closely by football, soccer, and kickball.

Richard was no exception as he enjoyed playing outdoor sports. During daily breaks from the private school sessions operated by his mother, he and the other young lads often engaged in outdoor physical activities. One of their popular sports was to organize a quick game of kickball. They could expend a lot of energy in a short period of time. Weather permitting, the spring and autumn seasons were ideal for their competitive games.

After all the boys rushed outside, Richard would gather them together in a semicircle to choose up sides. Many of the boys complained that the playing surface wasn't one of the spacious grassy areas that were located on all sides of the house. Richard always had the final say in such matters, and he preferred the gravelly surface of the long driveway.

His reason for playing on the surface made a lot of sense—the side boundaries were defined by the gravel itself. The width was approximately fifty feet. This way, there was absolutely no disputes on the out-of-bounds calls.

The game began similar to the start of a hockey game. A designated player would toss the ball from the side at midpoint between opposing kickers from each side. As in the game of soccer, hands were not allowed to be used. The primary difference between this version of kickball and soccer was that no established positions were utilized in kickball. It was simply a free-for-all affair. If the ball was in your vicinity, you kicked it.

Elbowing, shoving, and tripping were all part of the team's strategies to win. One morning when he was playing the game, Richard was tripped as he was trying to kick the ball. He fell forward on his knees and arms. His right elbow took the brunt of the fall. Several teammates rushed to his aid and helped him get on his feet. His elbow was gashed, and blood gushed from a three-inch cut below the elbow area. In addition, his hands were also skinned up. Two of his classmates helped him hobble toward the house as one of the boys hurried to fetch his mother.

"Now what?" Mrs. Warner declared as she greeted the boys on the front porch.

"We were playing kickball, and Richard fell and got a gash on his right elbow!" one of the boys piped up.

"And where were you boys playing?"

"On the driveway."

"No wonder! I've told you boys to always play on one of the grassy surfaces!"

"Yes, ma'am! But Richard—"

"Tommy, run into the kitchen and grab a kitchen towel for me! Quick!"

After she had wrapped the towel securely around his elbow she had a couple of the boys help him to the station wagon. Richard moaned and groaned on the short drive to the emergency room.

"Cut it out! You got what you deserved!" she admonished him.

"Well, well, look who we got here—my favorite patient!" the doc enthused.

Five stitches later, Richard was released.

On the way home, Richard's mom warned him that he was to sit outside of her office the rest of the day when he wasn't attending classes. She told him that if his elbow felt better, he could sit outside on the porch during break time the next couple of days.

Richard sat dejectedly on a lounge chair on the front porch the next morning during the first class break.

A couple of his classmates couldn't help but to tease him as they passed by.

"Ah, poor Richard can't play with us." One of them grinned.

"Yeah," another chimed in, "that's because he is chicken!"

"Am not!" Richard retorted.

The next morning, a similar scenario took place.

"Look, I'm a chicken!" Billy mocked as he flapped his arms up and down.

"Am not! I'll show you guys! Let's go!" Richard cried out as he got up from the lounge chair.

Some fifteen minutes later, history repeated itself, and Richard fell and tore the stiches apart.

When they arrived at the emergency room, Richard implored of his mother to help him inside.

"You decided you could play without my consent. Therefore, you can help yourself inside without my help!"

"I've been waiting for you, my boy!" The doctor grinned as he aided Richard into the operating room.

The stern look Richard's mom gave him as they made their way home sent shivers down his spine.

"The next week, we are going to tether you to a stake in the front of the house with one of your father's horse ropes!"

"Oh, please don't, Mom!"

"End of conversation!" she replied.

13

KAMP KILMAROCK

In 1953, the year Richard turned seventeen, his mother decided to start a day summer camp. Her private school was doing great—it was functioning at a capacity of 125 students. The camp would be called Kamp Kilmarock in honor of their new subdivision. It would be in session Monday through Friday from 9:00 a.m. to 5:00 p.m. The camp would be limited to fifty participants.

The proceeds from the camp would be used to help purchase one hundred new textbooks for the school. These books would be purchased from Simon & Schuster publishing firm.

Mrs. Warner's concept was to utilize the spacious two-plus acreage that their large three-story Victorian house stood on. The overall plan for this camp had been in the developmental stage for over two years. An Olympic-sized swimming pool had been installed on one side of the house, and a regulation tennis court sat due north of it. In the southeast corner of the property, a softball diamond had been built. In addition, a shuffleboard surface was put in place on one side of the front porch, and a game of badminton was set up on the other side. A horseshoe pit was placed in the rear of the house. An introduction to horseback riding and grooming would also be available.

Richard's dad, Harold, had purchased two older horses from the army's cavalry division for one dollar each. One end of their long wooden garage was converted into two stalls for the horses, and a hay rack was built nearby.

Several activities also took place in the huge basement of the house. A ping-pong table occupied one corner while several tables had been set up for various craft activities.

Richard was super excited as his mother had designated him as one of the camp counselors. She filled most of the counselor positions for the indoor activities with teachers who worked in her private school. In charge of the Olympic swimming pool, she hired a certified swimming instructor. And one of the local tennis pros from a nearby club gave tennis lessons on the tennis court.

The three activities Richard was assigned to work with were horseback riding, archery, and playing taps. He was very excited about the opportunity to be in a position of trust.

Every morning of camp began with Mrs. Warner and some of her teachers heading out in the school's station wagons to pick up the day campers. On the first day of camp, his mother assembled all the campers and counselors in front of the house.

"Welcome to Kamp Kilmarock! Our rules and regulations are easy to follow:

1. Listen to the instructions and commands your counselors give to you for the activities you will participate in.
2. We expect each of you to be on your best behavior at all times. You should report any injury or illness as soon as possible to your counselors. They will guide you to our infirmary inside the house located on the first floor. We have a registered nurse on duty.
3. We will assemble here every morning, and you will be dismissed with your counselor for the first activity of the day. At the conclusion of the day's activities, we will reassemble here for your rides back home.
4. You will rotate every hour from the activity of your choice to another. Each session will last approximately fifty minutes, with ten minutes' time to show up to your next activity. The school bell in the cupola of the kindergarten building will be rung to start and end each activity. This will give you ample time to go to the restrooms, which are also

located on the first floor of the house. Water will also be available at all times.

5.   The first thing on the agenda today is getting your Kamp Kilmarock T-shirts. They are orange and green in color, which are our private school colors. And they are emblazoned with the words KAMP KILMAROCK on the front. Your parents have already given us your sizes. I have three tables set up to your right. The first table has T-shirts on it for those of you who wear small sizes, the next table for medium sizes, and the third table for large sizes. You will reassemble here once you have received your camp T-shirts. I will then introduce you to each of the camp counselors and the activities they will be in charge of. Each of you has already made a list in the order of the activities you wish to participate in, so once your counselor and activity have been announced, you will follow them to the designated area.

We hope you have a wonderful summer
camp here at Kamp Kilmarock!"

Richard was anxious for his mother to introduce him as an assistant to Mrs. JoAnn Dingwell, who was in charge of the horse-riding activity. Five campers enthusiastically raised their hands and stepped forward to follow them to the horse stables.

When they reached the horse stables, Mrs. Dingwell addressed the campers, "We have two horses here on the Warner property, Bessie and Bonnie. They are older horses, and they are very tame. My assistant here, Richard Warner, will instruct you on the proper care and handling of the horses. Once in a while, I will take you in one of the school's station wagons to Pegasus Stables, where you will get to ride horses on supervised excursions on designated trails throughout Rock Creek Park. Richard will now introduce you to Bessie and Bonnie and inform you on how to safely deal with them."

"Okay," Richard said authoritatively as he slid open the large wooden door to the stables, "in the number 1 stall is Bessie, she is the female, and next to her in stall number 2 is Bonnie—he is the male horse."

"That's a funny name for a boy horse," one of the campers said.

"I agree." Richard nodded. "Whoever named him must have had too much apple cider to drink. Anyway, when you are approaching a horse for the first time, you want to be very calm and walk slowly. Talk to it in a soothing voice. Then grab a small handful of hay in one hand like this. Good morning, Bessie, would you like a little hay? Hold the hay a few inches in front of the horse's mouth for it to nibble on. Then you can very calmly begin to pet its forehead and stroke its neck.

"After a few minutes, you can grab the bridle and put it on the horse's head. The medal piece at the bottom of the bridle is simply called the bit. The first thing you will do is take these two long, thin leather straps called reins and place them over the horse's neck. Next, you hold the bridle up close to the horse's head. Take the medal bit and gently insert it into the horse's mouth. Finish by looping the bridle over the top of the horse's head. Then secure the leather strap fastener under its neck. I will lead Bessie out of her stall in front of the stables, and I will demonstrate some safety features for you. Now I'm going to tie the ends of the reins to the hitching post.

"Always approach your horse from the front or the side, preferably from the left side, as that is where we will mount the horse to ride it. Bessie is very tame and won't kick me, so I'm going to demonstrate for you."

He stepped behind Bessie and noted, "Never ever walk behind a horse as it could be very dangerous—" At that moment Bessie swished her tail to chase a horsefly away. The end of her tail caught Richard in the face.

The campers burst out laughing.

"Point well taken!" Mrs. Dingwell grinned.

A red-faced assistant stuttered, "Uh…next session we will talk about how to properly groom a horse."

After lunch, Richard had his archery activity, which was located near the softball diamond. For safety's sake, this activity was limited to six campers. A large circular target made out of thickly woven straw was placed on a sturdy easel. Each of the campers was given a bow. All the arrows which were equipped with blunt pointed tips and were located in a large cardboard box. The first shooting range was set at ten yards. Richard demonstrated how to properly hold the bow in one hand while getting the arrow ready to shoot with the other hand.

"Who wants to try it first?" he asked.

"I do!" the little redheaded girl shouted.

"Okay, here we go."

"Is this how I do it?"

"Whoa!" Richard warned as he grabbed the end of the arrow and bow in his hand. "This is a good lesson for you to learn, campers. Never, ever point any kind of weapon in the direction of another person."

The highlight of the camp for Richard was being able to play taps on a bugle at the conclusion of each week's sessions on Friday before the campers were taken home. He had received the bugle from his older brother Bobby. He taught him to play the bugle on family holidays.

Richard felt honored to play taps for the assembled campers.

14

LITTLE DRUMMER BOY

An integral part of Mrs. Warner's educational curriculum for her private school was the fine arts. She was very adamant that all her students became acquainted with and immersed in musical skills. Her students needed to know how to read sheet music and become familiar with and be able to play a musical instrument.

Richard was no exception. His mother insisted he learn how to play a piano. After several lessons and hours of practice time, he was becoming a competent pianist, but his heart wasn't really with becoming an accomplished pianist, and he hated the long hours of practice time that was required. However, he did perform well at a couple of recitals. His featured song at his first recital was the "Spinning Song," and at his second recital, the prominent song was "American Patrol."

About this time, he almost lost the tip of a finger in a lawn-mower accident. The difficulty in the adjustment he had to try to make in playing the piano with a stiff and crooked finger was the impetus he needed in trying some other musical instrument.

Richard had seen his brother William play drums for the George Washington University's band at a couple of concerts. He liked the sounds emanating from the drums his brother was playing, and he really enjoyed the physical activity involved. In addition, he liked the family's history relating to the drums. His grandfather had played drums for his military unit during the Civil War.

When he entered high school, he immediately enrolled in the band and signed up to play drums. Mrs. Warner was impressed with her son's dedication and enthusiasm for playing the drums.

She enrolled him in professional percussion lessons with a noted percussionist of the National Symphony of Washington, DC. Richard was schooled in playing all the percussion instruments. Percussion implies striking a surface with sticks to produce a sound. Besides drums, he was also able to play cymbals, a xylophone, a marimba, and a triangle—to name a few. Encouraged by his mother and some of the professionals he had worked with, he auditioned for the National Symphony, but he didn't make the cut.

These lessons from the professional percussionist enabled him to not only secure first chair in the drum section of his high school band, but also to fill in when necessary with the other percussion instruments. During this time of training and playing, Richard discovered twenty-six rudiments of drum playing.

His dad actually helped him secure his first professional gig with the Montgomery County Symphony under the direction of Chester Petronic, but all Richard was ever assigned to play was the cymbals. After six months, he resigned from the symphony because he found it to be too boring.

Although his high school days kept him quite busy with his academic pursuits and his involvement with the band, he still found time to play with various local bands on the weekends.

He would continue playing drums while serving in the military. While undergoing flight training for the navy in the Pensacola, Florida, Richard was able to secure the position of first chair drummer with the US Naval Aviation Cadet Band under the direction of Chief Master Sergeant Art Symington.

Richard appreciated Chief Master Sergeant Symington because of his common-sense approach to his music, the military, and life in general. This military band not only marched in military parades, but they also performed in such parade events as the Gasparilla Pirate Festival in Tampa, Florida, and in the Orange Bowl located in Miami.

Richard was pleased that a military building in the Pensacola area was named after his good friend and mentor Chief Master Sergeant Art Symington.

In addition, he also performed with a military band that often played at the local NCO Clubs.

15

APPRENTICESHIP AT HOT SHOPPES

At the end of his eighth-grade schooling at his mother's private school, Richard was informed that it was now time for him to work outside of the home and earn his own spending money as he prepared to enter high school. Secretly, he was thrilled. Now he could discover his manhood on his own terms without the watchful scrutiny of his mother and father.

"Where am I going to find work?" he queried his parents.

"We think we know the right place for you to begin working this summer," his mother informed him.

"As you are aware of, Richard, your father and I occasionally dine out a place called the Hot Shoppes. We have become acquainted with the owner, Mr. Jay Willard Marriott. Upon inquiry as to job openings, he told us about available car hop positions for their outside food service. We mentioned to him that you were looking for summer employment, and he advised us to send you over for an interview."

"Wow! That sounds exciting!" he enthused.

"Richard, remember your actions will reflect on the Warner household. Make sure you are groomed properly and dressed in your best work attire. And always, always, be prompt! Be polite and courteous to you customers and fellow employees."

"Yes, ma'am!"

"Your interview is tomorrow morning at nine with Mrs. Weidner."

Richard arrived promptly at Hot Shoppes for his interview at 8:50 a.m. Upon entering the restaurant, he was directed to Mrs. Weidner's office.

"Come on in, young man," she commanded him. "I've been expecting you."

"Thank you, ma'am," he said hesitantly as he entered her office.

Rising from her chair, she rounded her desk and stood face-to-face with Richard. She scrutinized him from head to toe and had him do a 360-degree turn for inspection. She then had him hold out his hands, which she inspected carefully. "Young man, I am impressed! You were prompt for your interview, your clothing is appropriate and clean, you are well groomed, and your shoes are shined! Do you brush your teeth?"

"Yes, ma'am, morning and night," he replied.

"Good! You will begin work at eleven tomorrow morning. One of our regular car hops will show the routine. And one other thing you need to be aware of, young man, any violation of the above rules will result in a one-day's suspension without pay. A second violation will necessitate dismissal."

Richard was very enterprising from the get-go as he wanted to be the best car hop at Hot Shoppes. He quickly memorized all the items on the menu, and he soon discovered from his interaction with the customers what their favorites where. It wasn't unusual for him to greet many of his repeat customers with, "Will you be having the usual today, sir/ma'am?"

Before long, some of them would request for him to wait on them. He was also very careful not to interfere with or bad-mouth any of the other car hops. He went out of his way to offer his assistance should they request it.

In a short amount of time the owner, Mr. Jay Willard Marriott became aware of this industrious young man, and he invited Richard in for an informal interview. "Young man, I'm very impressed with your work ethic. How would you like to become a waiter for me here inside the restaurant?"

"Yes, sir, that sounds great!"

"You will wear a uniform consisting of the following: black trousers that have a distinctive purple stripe down the sides of the legs, a full-sleeved white shirt, red bow tie, red cummerbund, a white dinner jacket, and black shoes—which you must supply—and they must be highly polished."

"Yes, sir!"

"Your pay will be two dollars a day, plus tips."

"Wow!"

"Do you have any questions?"

"Good! Go see Mrs. Weidner. She will get the measurements for your uniform. You will begin your duties as a waiter next Monday. Until then, you will continue with your car hop chores."

In addition to the two-dollar-a-day pay, Richard was able to earn twenty-five to thirty dollars from tips because of his enthusiasm, his knowledge of the menu items, and his people skills. The actual money he earned on a daily basis often surpassed what his father, a college professor, probably made.

Richard's boss, Jay Willard Marriott, would increase his businesses to include hotels. His grandson would take the Marriott hotel chain public.

The next summer, Richard opted to become an apprentice as a brick mason.

16

FIRST CAR: A 1941 BUICK COUPE

Richard was adamant. He was sixteen years old in 1952, and he was bound and determined to buy his first car because he had saved enough money from working for the brick masons to buy a used vehicle. His father wasn't too pleased with the idea, but he had to acquiesce to his son's determination to buy a car because he had earned the money, for one.

It didn't take long for him to discover a good used car that struck his fancy. The car in question was a 1941 Buick Coupe. The vehicle was black in color with a silver top—very sporty looking! But the real selling point for Richard was the interior of the car. The showpiece was the white pearl steering wheel. An unusual but catchy feature was the starter, which was located under the accelerator pedal. Surprisingly, the radio was in good shape. It was the basic model USA-230. He liked utilizing the standard shifting transmission, and he was happy with the straight-eight engine, which had an output of 165 horsepower, which in 1941 was the highest rated of any American automobile. And the best news? The price! It was only two hundred and ninety-five dollars!

Richard was really anxious to try out his prized possession, the 1941 Buick Coupe. With much coaxing and pleading, he convinced his begrudging parents to let him visit his uncle Jewel and aunt Elsa Boch in Wynnewood, Pennsylvania, a plush neighborhood in Philadelphia. He was excited by the trip because his uncle was really into the Buick cars.

It was basically a day's drive to his uncle and aunt's home in Philly. This gave Richard ample time to really become familiar with his car. With the radio blaring some of his favorite tunes, he boldly accelerated on long stretches of the highway. pretending he was a famous Indy driver. He was so caught up in the performance of his new car that he only stopped for fuel and using the restroom facilities.

The first order of business for Richard after arriving at Uncle Jewel and Elsa's home and giving them the necessary hugs and greetings was to show off his vehicle to his uncle. His uncle Jewel complimented him on his choice of a Buick car and told him they were the most reliable car in the country. He then proceeded to show off his Buick cars to Richard.

Richard was totally enthralled with his uncle Jewel. His uncle had made his fortune in the real estate business in Philly. He was a noted philanthropist for his many charitable works in the area. And he was a definite workaholic with a definite genius for woodworking. He had a huge lathe, and he designed and made all the furniture for their house. Richard was mesmerized with the skill his uncle displayed in his large woodworking shop.

But it wasn't all work and no play with his Uncle. One evening after a sumptuous dinner, his uncle invited him to his private den. "Young man, I'm impressed with your pleasant manners and your willingness to help out. You are well-disciplined, and you listen to what I say without interrupting me. Therefore, you have earned the right to enjoy a beer with me. Join me with a toast with my favorite German beer!"

"Thank you, Uncle Jewel!" Richard enthused.

The week went by too swiftly, and Richard was soon motoring down the road for home. Sadly, eleven months later his father coerced him into selling his first car. He did get back the money he had invested in it, however.

17

PENN STATE UNIVERSITY

At the conclusion of his high school years, Richard was seriously contemplating on following in his brother Billy's footsteps and joining the navy. However, his mother wanted him to attend a four-year college/university of his own choosing. As most mothers often react, she abhorred the idea of another son in the military.

So he begrudgingly gave into his mother's wishes. She promised him they would pay for his first year of school if he would work at home, taking care of the outside chores such as feeding the horses, Bessie and Bonnie, cleaning their stalls, exterminating the rats in the barn, mowing the lawn, and running errands.

One of the educational areas Penn State was noted for was its forestry department. Because of his fascination with the family's variety of fruit trees and the neighbor's forty-five acres of different types of trees, Richard decided to enroll at Penn State University. His focus would be on dendrology, which is a study of trees.

In a class on the study of tree leaves, he became very adept at identifying the leaves by their color, shape, and vein patterns. He also enjoyed the outdoors, where they utilized a number of techniques and apparatus to determine the height and girth of a tree, calibrate the board feet of a tree, and to identify the age of a tree by counting its concentric rings.

Another class that held his undivided attention dealt with mensuration, which focused on measurements. They measured land acreage and learned the concept of drawing maps.

He had difficulty with his chemistry class but did manage to get a passing grade in it. However, he failed his English class, which caused him to be placed on probation for the next semester. Ironically the problem was he had an innate fear of presenting an oral report in front of the class. His instructor had warned him that a passing grade hinged on his oral delivery of the report.

During his first year at Penn State, he formed a close-knit bond with a number of the other students. And for entertainment, they often devised devious pranks to pull on unsuspecting people. Richard was involved in two of their most memorable pranks. One of the most popular make-out spots for the young college couples was located off an old logging trail in one of the nearby hills. His friends gathered around in his room one Friday evening following a week of classes. Due to a rather hectic week of tests, they were primed to let off some steam.

"Okay," Tommy interjected, "who are we going to surprise this week?"

"Hey, I know," Charley chimed in," let's do something to some of our college love bugs!"

"Great idea!" Ralph exclaimed. "Anybody have a plan?"

"I've got the perfect plan," Richard announced.

"Well, let's hear it," they demanded.

"Okay, guys, this is what we are going to do. We will back in near a small of grove of trees some two hundred feet on a minor logging trail below the couple's parked vehicle. This way we'll have a fast getaway if we need it."

"So what are we going to do?" Tommy asked.

"I learned a great military tactic from my older my brother Billy, who is in the navy—divide and conquer!"

"How is that going to work," Charley added.

"Here are the details of the plan, gentlemen. After we park our getaway vehicle, we will quietly and quickly divide into four prongs of attack. Tommy, you will sneak up on the front passenger side of the car. Charley, you will approach the driver's side of the car. Ralph, you will have the rear passenger side. I've got the rear driver's side of the car. Once we are safely hidden and in position from our designated targets, I will give a signal of the sound of a hooting owl. We will then, in a low crouching position, approach our targets. We will kneel in front of our tires and quickly remove the metal caps on the air valves. Next, we reverse the caps and start to unscrew the valve stems until we hear the air hissing out from the tire. As soon as this happens, we drop the cap and run for the nearest cover of trees. Then we make a beeline for the car and get the heck out of Dodge!"

"Let's do it!" they enthused.

They were right in the middle of pulling off a successful prank when they heard a loud exclamation coming from the car, "What the hell is going on out there!"

"Run for it!" Richard shouted out.

A couple of shotgun blasts rang out as they panicked and ducked behind the nearest available cover.

Their most sadistic and daring prank took place a few weeks later. Ralph, who had a tendency to walk on the wild side, presented his morbid plan to the group. There was a somewhat tame alley cat that prowled the campus grounds. He would capture the cat by luring it with a piece of meat and then enclose it in a burlap sack. "I will then take it behind that abandoned old house near the west side of the campus. I will grab the cat out of the bag, slit its throat with my pocketknife, and then squeeze its blood into a small sealable plastic container. After that, I will place the cat's remains back in the burlap and dump in the nearest trash receptacle."

"That's terrible!" Richard uttered, suddenly feeling nauseous.

"And then what!" Charley said somewhat hesitantly.

"Here is the exciting part of the plan," Ralph affirmed, "we are going to fake a murder on the Main Street downtown!"

"Let's do it!" Tommy said excitedly.

"Okay, this is the way it is going to work," Ralph instructed. "We will take my dad's WWII jeep. Charley will be the designated driver. He will let Tommy and me off at the corner of Main and Vine. Because Tommy is the smallest of the group, he will be wearing a white T-shirt with the plastic bag containing the cat's blood taped to his chest. As a member of the track team, I will procure a starter's pistol and a blank shell from our coach. I will have this starter gun tucked away in my front pocket. We will all be wearing our black trench coats and dark stocking caps to avoid being recognized. Tommy and I will slowly walk down the street pretending to be in a heated argument. In the meantime, Charley, you will have already driven around the block and back onto Main Street. Tommy and I will get into a brief shouting and shoving match, then I will withdraw the pistol and shoot Tommy, and then I will flee around the block and out of sight. Tommy will give a dramatic dying performance as he clutches and breaks the plastic bag. At the sound of the starter gun firing, Charley, you and Richard will speed up to help the fallen victim. Once you are along the side of Tommy, you will immediately apply the emergency brake, and then you and Richard will jump out of the jeep, pick up Tommy, and hoist him into the back of the jeep. Then you will speed around the block and pick me up."

The prank actually worked! Some terrified bystanders eventually found a city policeman and directed him to the sight of the fake shooting. A radio broadcast later announced the suspicious shooting that had supposedly occurred on their nightly addition of the news. A sample of the blood taken from the sidewalk was shipped to a nearby lab for analysis. The results clearly indicated that it was some sort of animal blood. The local newspaper indicated the probability that it was a college prank.

On a more charitable note, Richard had volunteered to drive a dozen students to Sunday morning church services at the Christian Science Church that was located downtown. He drove one of the university's old trucks that had wooden benches secured in the back of it. On his first trip there, Richard was smitten by the church's sign, which proclaimed, "God is Love, Love is God."

Because his father was upset with his failing grade in English, Richard was compelled to take an English course at nearby Georgetown University that summer. When asked how he did in the course, he replied that he had received a gentleman's C.

18

BUT, MOM, UNCLE SAM WANTS ME...

Most young boys growing up in their formative years had heroes that they idolized—from comic book heroes such as Superman, Spiderman, and the Green Hornet to sports athletes like Babe Ruth, Lou Gehrig, and Ted Williams, and of course, movie stars like John Wayne, Burt Lancaster, and Henry Fonda.

Richard was no exception. However, his hero was his older brother, William (Billy) Warner. At holiday gatherings, he could listen for hours as Billy told him of his experiences in the navy. And Billy was very patient in answering the myriad questions that Richard bombarded him with.

When Richard was nearing his high school graduation in 1954, his brother Billy encouraged him to give a great deal of thought to joining one of the armed services—specifically the navy.

Early one evening, Richard approached his mother privately in the kitchen. "Mom, can I visit with you about what I'm planning on doing following my graduation?"

"Why, of course you can, son. What's on your mind?"

"Well, I've been thinking about maybe joining the navy."

"Oh, no you don't! I bet your brother Billy put you up to this!"

"Kind of, but I really think I'd like it."

"Listen here, young man! I've told you several times that you are going to college. There are several good Catholic colleges you can choose from. And I'll not only let you pick the one you want to go to, but I'll help you get enrolled."

"No, Mom, I've made up my mind!" He turned and stomped out of the kitchen.

"Richard, you listen to me, you hear!" Her admonitions trailed away as he hurriedly ascended the stairwell to his room.

His decision to join the navy was confirmed in June 1954 when he visited his brother, Lt. Commander William Warner's ship, the *Calvin Coolidge*. The naval band was dressed out in full regalia, blaring out the navy song and other patriotic tunes. Richard was fired up! The next day he went down to the nearest naval recruiting station and enlisted as a navy ET.

His basic training took place in nearby Anacostia in Washington, DC. Although the training was rigorous, it posed no difficulty for Richard to manage. He was used to hard work and obeying orders at home and in school. In addition, he was an accomplished swimmer—thanks to the family's Olympic-sized swimming pool, so one of the biggest hurdles for many of the recruits was a piece of cake for him. Of course, the one thing he detested was the instructor hollering in his face. Even though he later understood this technique utilized by the armed services during basic training, he still believed there was a better approach.

Following a brief leave of absence after basic training, Richard's advanced individual training was also held at Anacostia. His military occupation code was an ad striker. The focus of this program was in the maintenance field.

After the advanced training was completed. his first assignment was to attend a three months cooking school. Besides attending classes, he was also assigned some cooking and cleaning duties.

One of the navy chiefs he became friends with encouraged him to take the Navcad test. Richard scored very high on the test and was called in for questioning.

"Mr. Warner, you have scored so high on the Navcad test that we are going to offer you two excellent possibilities for you to think about. Both are great career opportunities, but of course the navy hopes you pick the first one. Young man, you have been selected to go to the Naval Academy at Annapolis. Your second option—which would also be an outstanding career choice—would be to attend

Naval aviator training in Pensacola, Florida. I realize this is a big decision, so think it over carefully and give me your answer at 0800 hours tomorrow. Dismissed."

Knock. Knock.

"Come on in. Well, Mr. Warner, what is your decision?"

"Sir, I've decided on aviator school in Pensacola."

"Good choice! I'll write up your shipping orders. Be ready to report there in two weeks!"

"Thank you, sir!"

"Good luck, young man!"

19

1950 PONTIAC COUPE

Although the Warner family was disappointed that Richard didn't select the naval academy at Annapolis to pursue his career, his father, Harold, offered to drive him to Pensacola, Florida, in his 1950 Pontiac gray two-door Coupe.

Richard's mom prepared a splendid feast for him the evening before his departure. The family enjoyed reminiscing about the days growing up in the old Victorian house. Of course, he was the focal point of their recollections.

Richard awoke early the next morning eager to take the next step in his life's journey. Following a hearty breakfast consisting of eggs, bacon, hash browns, hotcakes and an assortment of fruit it was time to depart. Tearful hugs and goodbyes were exchanged all around. However, saying goodbye to his mother proved to be the most difficult. She had been the strong presence and leader of the Warner family, so leaving the embrace of this most powerful influence in his life was very sad.

His father waited patiently at the front door for him. He had already loaded Richard's duffel bag with several goodies his mother had prepared for him. Finally, at his father's urging, he tore himself away from his mother's embrace, and with tears streaming down his face, he bolted for the car.

Richard sat sobbing in the passenger side of the car with his head in his hands. His dad eased the car slowly down the driveway and onto the street. By the time Richard had gained control of his emotions, they were already exiting the Washington, DC, area.

The trip down to Pensacola, Florida, was fascinating to him. He was enthralled with the beauty of the changing landscape as they headed south down US Highway 29. With so much scenery to take in, it was difficult focusing on the growing-up wisdom his dad was imparting to him.

"Did you hear what I was just telling you?"

"Yeah, of course, Dad."

"Well, you didn't seem to be paying attention to me. Tell me, what did I have to say?"

"Huh, let's see. I know, you were telling me about things I should and shouldn't do, like having good hygiene."

"Okay, I guess maybe you were."

Richard was so focused on getting to Pensacola that the trip seemed like a blur. He did remember that the trip was 1,200 miles long, and it took three days to travel by car. Highway 29 was a two-lane highway and passed through several small towns. He did recall that they always stayed at a Howard Johnson's motel. This popular chain of motels was known for its unique appearance and restaurant facilities. And, Dr. Warner was very fond of their ice cream. Chocolate was a favorite of his, and he was known to devour a quart of it in a single sitting.

The father and son's conversations on the three-day trip were basically one-sided. After starting each day trying to engage his son in a variety of topics that he thought might interest him, he gave into his son's silence and let the radio do the talking.

Midafternoon on the third day, they finally arrived at the naval aviator station in Pensacola. After checking in and presenting his official orders, Richard was told to report at 0900 hours the next day.

Harold and his son then checked into another Howard Johnson's for the evening. Before they had their meal, they made a brief journey to the Pensacola airport, and his dad made reservations for a flight back to Washington, DC, on Eastern Airlines. His flight was scheduled for the next morning at eight. This would be ample time for Richard to take his dad to the airport and then make his check in at the base.

Besides the thrill of arriving in Pensacola to begin his aviator training, Richard was excited to be getting his very own car. His dad was selling him the 1950 Pontiac Coupe for the sum of $400.

At the airport the next morning, his dad gave him a firm handshake and then handed him the keys to the car. Richard hurried to the car, hopped in the driver's seat, and placed his hands firmly on the steering wheel.

"I got wheels now, and I'm my own man!" he proclaimed.

20

I'M IN LOVE!

The excitement of being admitted to flight school in Pensacola was dimmed somewhat by the waiting game that many enlisted men in the armed forces had to deal with. On his arrival, Richard had been assigned maintenance duties on the base, which was in keeping with his original MOS training. After two weeks of this routine duty, he was beginning to get a little worried.

However, this duty was made more bearable by the friendship he developed with a navy seaman, William Seiple, who was a three stripper and an airman apprentice. Richard's fascination with this young man was because he appeared to be a self-assured man of the world. William was very smooth with the young ladies. He seemed to revel in telling Richard about his many escapades. Richard was silently jealous.

One afternoon when they had break time from one of their assigned duties for the day, Seaman William confronted Richard about his lack of a love life. "Man, you got to get with the program! I'm beginning to get worried about you!"

"Hey, I've only been here for a couple of weeks!"

"Doesn't make any difference. You got to go out and search for the available sweethearts! After all, they aren't going to come looking for you!"

"I'll get to it pretty soon."

"Oh, sure you will! I'll tell you what, I'm going to fix you up with a blind date. I had a date recently with a pretty young lady. She's young, only sixteen years old. A friend of mine set me up with her, and we had a date to go roller skating, which by the way, she is really good at. Anyway, the point is, she is kind of a standoffish girl—you know, pretty straitlaced. Come to think of it Richard, kind of like you are." He laughed.

"You say she's pretty?"

"Yeah, real pretty."

"Well, yeah, I'd probably be interested in meeting her."

"I think I can get her phone number from my friend, and we'll see if we can set you up with a blind date."

"Okay, huh, by the way, what's her name?"

"Well, her first name is sort of unusual. Her name is Druwanda Woolam."

"Boy, that's different!"

"Yeah, but like I said, she's a looker!"

Richard was intrigued! Not only was she supposedly good looking, but her name was so exotic!

He was so excited he couldn't sleep that night. He tossed and turned with visions of this angelic young lady floating in his mind. Finally, the sound of revelry, it was time to rise and shine. He barely touched his breakfast. He couldn't wait for his daily work assignment with William to begin.

"Hey, Seaman, what did you find out?"

"Whoa, boy! Look, I had a date last night. I haven't had time to arrange it."

"Huh, okay," a dejected young man replied.

"Hey, don't be so dopey. Are you lovesick already? You haven't even met her yet!" He laughed. "But I promise you, I'll get on it right away."

The next morning, Seaman William had good news for Richard. "You will get to meet and date the girl of your dreams Saturday at 1800 hours. You will pick her up at her house. Do not knock, just ring the doorbell."

"Where does she live?"

"Take it easy! I have her address written down for you on this slip of paper." He fished it out of his shirt pocket and handed it to him.

Richard quickly scanned the note. Druwanda's address was 1322 Dexter Avenue, Warrington, Florida, which was a nearby suburb of Pensacola. In a matter of seconds, he had her address committed to memory.

It was only Thursday, so the next couple of days were an eternity to him. At precisely 1800 hours, Richard rang the doorbell. He looked very military in his navy dress uniform.

The door opened abruptly.

"Who is it?" a curiously dressed young woman asked.

"I'm Richard Warner."

"Why, of course! We've been expecting you! Please come in!"

As she quickly led him to a sofa in the spacious living room, Richard couldn't help thinking, not only how foxy this young woman looked but how mature she seemed to be.

"Have a seat, young man, and tell me a little bit about yourself."

"Huh, well, I…"

At that moment, a very striking young girl descended a nearby staircase. "Hi, my name is Druwanda! I see you've met my mother, Christine."

"Uh, yes I did."

He would learn later that Druwanda's mother was only thirty-three years old.

With an awkward "thank you" to her mother, Richard escorted Druwanda to his 1950 Pontiac Coupe. For their first date, he treated her to a movie at a nearby theater.

It was most definitely *love at first sight*!

21

BOOT CAMP (ALL OVER AGAIN)

Richard's aviator ground school training class was supposed to have begun in January 1956. The officer in charge of the maintenance unit that he had been attached to finally informed him that his aviator training would officially begin in a few weeks in February. He would begin training with Class 656 George Company. The first number, 6, stood for the actual sixth class of this aviator training. The second and third numbers represented the year 1956.

There were forty-eight naval enlisted men in George Company 656. The attrition rate of this class was high. Fifty percent dropped out during the four month's class. Those wishing to drop out were required to fill out a DOR form, which was a dropout request form. These requests were usually granted. Richard surmised that most of these young men didn't like the physical demands of the boot camp portion of the training.

Richard's orders were for him to report at 0600 hours on Monday in front of Building 633. This building was where the majority of the aviator ground school classes would be conducted.

At the required time of the 0600 hours formation, the forty-eight young men were called to attention by some loud, fierce-looking marine drill instructor, more commonly referred to as DIs. The DIs gave them orders regarding the time of the morning and evening formations, expected dress uniforms, schedule of daily and weekly events to follow, and proper behavior.

The naval trainees were then marched to a nearby barracks. Here they were issued bedding and necessary toiletry items. They were assigned eight to a room that contained four double bunk beds. The naval cadet who was designated the battalion commander and senior class officer was Ed Nixon. He was the twenty-year younger brother of future president Richard M. Nixon.

Once they were settled in, the Marine DI then marched them to Building 633 to begin their ground school training. Richard found the various classes to be quite interesting. He was impressed with the various parts of the plane and the functions performed by such necessary parts as wing flaps, tail sections, and the rudder, to name a few. The lift and wing dynamics simply amazed him.

Richard really excelled in the class that dealt with the mechanics of the plane's engine. An actual split engine was on hand for inspection and study. He had helped his dad and brother work on the truck and car engines when he was growing up in DC, so he was always volunteering relevant information regarding the functions of an engine as well as helping to demonstrate the workings of key components of an engine.

The boot training portion of the class was tough and demanding, but Richard had no problems with the physical aspects of it. He was in good shape and enjoyed the competition. Richard enjoyed the order and discipline of military formations and marches. Every morning after formation and roll call, the marines drill instructor, Sergeant Duckworth, would march the trainees to their first class. "Company, ten-hut! Right face! For'd Harch!"

He liked the give-and-take of the marching cadence.

"I don't know, but I've been told!"

"I don't know, but I've been told!"

"Company G is passing by!"

"Company G is passing by!"

The Marine DI's liked Richard's guttural tone of voice when he responded to the cadence call. Early one morning after formation and roll call, the D I shouted out, "Trainee Warner!"

"Yes, Sergeant!" he responded.

"Front and center!"

"Yes, Sergeant!"

Richard took a step forward. Because of his short height, he was put in the first row. He then did a left face, took three steps, did a right face, and marched forward until he was face-to-face with the DI.

"Trainee Warner!"

"Yes, Sergeant!"

"You will march the trainees to class today!"

"Yes, Sergeant!"

Richard did a rear pivot move and faced the company.

"Company, ten-hut! Right face! For'd Harch!

"Hut, two, three, four!"

"Hut, two, three, four!"

He felt honored, he was in charge! Consequently, the DI often called him out to lead the march.

Some of the trainees obviously weren't too thrilled when they learned that they were going to have to go through a very demanding obstacle course twice every week during the four months' class. The course consisted of running over a hilly up-and-down trail, to several different climbing and challenging obstacles, to swinging on ropes to crossing water hazards, to belly crawling under barbed wire, and to physically jousting with each other with padded poles.

The culmination of the boot camp was one week of survival training in a densely wooded area. None of the aviator trainees knew of this area they would be dropped off in. They were each given only the very necessary simple tools to survive with. The primary focal point of this survival training was for the trainees to be able to utilize their own unique talents and skills in conjunction with the other members of their team. Bloated egos had to be set aside for the training to function properly.

A highlight of this week of training was when one of the trainees had successfully captured a young rabbit. The rabbit stew they concocted that evening was delicious!

Other than pesky flying insects to deal with, the biggest physical threat came from scorpions. The trainees soon learned to have each other's backs during survival week. A couple of the young men were stung by these little creatures. Fortunately, they weren't of the highly poisonous variety. The bite of the scorpions was comparable to that of bees.

Actually, the biggest complaint Richard had during this four months' training was not being able to see his new girlfriend, Druwanda, enough. However, he was able to secure a few weekend passes because of good performances in class and during boot training. The highlight of these dates was usually attending a movie together.

At the conclusion of the four-month aviator ground school course and boot camp, the rank of those trainees who successfully completed the course was posted.

Richard was delighted to see that he ranked in the top 10 percent of his class.

22

WHITING FIELD

"Cadet Warner!"

"Yes, sir!"

"Now that you have successfully completed the first step in your quest to become a pilot by your outstanding achievements in aviator ground school, you are being transferred to Whiting Field in Milton, Florida, which is only twenty-five miles due north of here. Your primary training will begin there in the T34B plane."

"What time do I need to report there, sir?"

"At 0800 hours tomorrow, Cadet."

"Uh, okay, thank you, sir."

"Good luck, son."

Even though Richard was super excited to finally begin flying, he was disappointed he would only have a brief evening to spend with Druwanda. He was becoming very attached to this pretty young lady, who was now seventeen and a junior in high school.

But he was thrilled to report in at 0800 hours the next day at Whiting Field.

"Cadet Warner reporting for duty, sir!"

"Well, Cadet, check in at supply and pick up your bedding and necessary items. Then you will take your items to Barrack C24. Hold on a second, let me check my roommates' list here. Ah, yes, you will be rooming with Cadet Roy Marshall. Dismissed."

"Thank you, sir!" Richard left the reporting station, picked up his supplies, and headed for Barrack C24. He was surprised to see that Cadet Roy Marshall was already making up his own bed.

"Hello, my name is Richard Warner. I guess we will be roomies."

"Hey, glad to meet you! My name is Roy Marshall." He gave Richard a firm handshake and asked him if he needed any help getting settled in.

"No," he said. He liked the personality of the young man right away. While they were unpacking and making their beds, they exchanged information about their immediate goals regarding flying, their families, and where they were from. Richard was impressed when Cadet Marshall revealed that he was from California.

The next morning, Richard introduced himself to his flight instructor, Marine Captain Rudy Bolves. He instinctively knew that Captain Bolves was a no-nonsense kind of guy.

"Well, Cadet Warner, we are going to get started right away. Pick up your flight suit and get changed in the locker room down the hall on your right and then report back here to me."

"Yes, sir!"

Once he had changed into his flight suit, he followed Captain Bolves to Hangar 3 for preflight inspection of the T34B plane they would be flying that day.

After the inspection, they prepared to board the plane. "By the way, Cadet Warner, have you ever flown in an airplane?"

"Oh, yes, sir! My brother flies for the navy, and I was able to fly with him!"

"So flying doesn't bother you at all?"

"No, sir, I thoroughly enjoy it!"

"Okay, climb aboard, let's get going!"

Captain Bolves guided the T34B down the runway for a smooth lift off. Suddenly he put the T34B into a huge upside-down aerial loop. As the plane was coming out of the loop, he took it straight up for several hundred feet, then aimed the plane downward in a steep dive. Richard was setting behind Captain Bolves in this two-seat trainer, and he lost it. He threw up all over himself and the interior of the plane.

When Captain Bolves brought the plane in for a landing, Richard was concerned about the repercussions he would face because of his puking all over the plane. The interior of the plane had a sickening smell to it.

After they disembarked from the plane, Captain Bolves addressed a pale-faced and shaking young cadet. "Well, Cadet, as you declared, you're an experienced flyer. Now go change your uniform, clean yourself up, and report back to the hangar. You have a plane to clean up!"

"Y-yes, yes, sir!"

Some three hours later, the cleaning and disinfecting of the plane was completed. Richard was given a valuable lesson on the unexpected extremes of flying that would serve him well into the future.

One morning as they headed out for their preflight inspection of the plane, Richard hurried ahead of the captain to begin the inspection.

"Cadet Warner!"

Richard stopped abruptly in his tracks. "Yes, sir!"

"Front and center, Cadet, now!"

"Yes, sir, Captain!"

"Cadet Warner, you never ever jump out ahead of a marine officer!"

"Yes, sir!"

"You know you are to stay one-half of a pace behind me on my left side!"

"Right, sir!"

"And don't you ever forget it, young man!"

"Sir, yes, sir!"

On his ninth flight scheduled for June 11, 1957, Richard was informed that he was to perform his first solo flight. He was excited and scared at the same time; he wouldn't have his safety blanket, Captain Bolves, sitting behind him. However, once he successfully lifted off from the grassy field, he was exhilarated and in total control of the plane. He did the required loop around the perimeter of the field and brought the plane in for a smooth landing.

The three months' training from June to August 1957 went by quickly. Richard's final test was a solo flight that involved several touch-and-gos. This maneuver consisted of lightly touching down as if landing and then lifting off into the air again.

Cadet Warner was excited! He was now flying! The only negative aspect was only getting to visit with Druwanda for one evening.

23

CORRY NAVAL AIR STATION

Cadet Warner was transferred back to the Pensacola area to Corry Naval Air Station, which was located three miles up the road from the main gate of Pensacola Naval Air Station.

In this second step of military pilot training, he transitioned from the T34B plane to the T28B plane. Its prominent feature was a huge propeller. This plane was subsequently replaced by the T28C model, which featured a smaller propeller.

The main thrust of this training was for the cadets to learn to fly-in formation. On his first flight, Richard's instructor demonstrated the proper flying technique to maneuver from the side and below the aircraft to join in formation.

"Okay, Cadet Warner, this morning you will successfully join up with another plane in formation. Any questions?"

"Huh, no, sir!"

Richard was nervous about trying this procedure for the first time. He attempted to accomplish the wing tip to wing tip maneuver by working the rudder pedals only; however, the wing wasn't in proper trim. His instructor, sitting behind him, grabbed the flying stick and shouted, "I've got it!"

Richard knew the correct response and immediately threw his arms up in the air.

To prove a point, the instructor initiated a tight maneuver and rubbed the tip of their plane against the tip of the other plane. This served a twofold function: it helped alleviate the fear of the close encounter and emphasized the importance of the proper approach with correct wing trim. Richard discovered the closer you were to your plane in the formation, the easier it was.

His roommate during this training was Larry Bagwell from Clemson, South Carolina. He became friends with Larry during their ground school classes. Cadet Bagwell appeared to be a typical all-American boy. He was fun to be around, and he seemed to handle the stress of the training with no apparent problems. He never complained and was always ready to go.

On the morning he was designated to take his solo flight, the weather was good. After successfully performing a few of the required maneuvers, he suddenly took the plane up in a vertical path, and then, for whatever reason, the plane went into a straight nosedive into the grassy field. Cadet Bagwell died immediately. All the pieces and parts of the plane were gathered up and taken to a vacant hangar. All that could be officially determined was that the plane had impacted at three hundred knots.

There was speculation that Larry may have taken his own life. However, Cadet Bagwell had seemed in good spirits that morning and was eager to take his solo flight. No notes or letters were left behind, and no one could recall any negative conversations with him.

Unfortunately, two days later when night flying touch-and-go maneuvers were being practiced, a cadet coming in for the brief touchdown had the pitch of the large propeller at the wrong angle, causing the engine to burst, and it killed him.

Ironically neither of the two terrible accidents seemed to have an emotional effect on Richard. Two weeks later, he flew his solo and formation final by joining the formation at Four Silo Farms.

Richard was happy during this period of his aviator training. He was able to spend some time most every evening with Druwanda. He would join her and her family for dinner and then relax watching TV. Occasionally they would go to a drive-in movie theater. As their relationship grew so did their petting and kissing. Druwanda was always decked out in a nicely starched dress, so as a consequence of their making out at the drive-in theater, the dress was usually quite wrinkled when he took her home. He worried that her parents might come to the wrong conclusion about their relationship.

This training session covered the September to November time frame. Richard was ready for step 3: Bearon Field!

24

BARIN FIELD

The transfer to Barin Field took place in December 1956. Richard and the other cadets who had successfully completed Step Two at Corry Naval Air Station arrived at Barin Field, which was located fifty miles due north of Pensacola across the border in Foley, Alabama. These young men would soon learn why this place was aptly termed, Bloody Barin Field. Several would-be-pilots would lose their lives during this step of the training.

The object of this three-month training session was to fly the SNJ (T6) which was equipped with a tail wheel dragger. They would practice carrier landing on a dry field before attempting to land on a real floating carrier ship. However, this solo attempt at landing on a carrier ship at sea was postponed because the nearest available carrier was currently out of commission.

One of the casualties during this training period was his room-mate, Bob Shirley. On a critical field carrier landing attempt Cadet Shirley came in too low and too slow, which caused his plane to crash shy of the designated landing area, resulting in his death. All cadets had been warned about this danger with this plane. The landing had to be accomplished with the plane at the proper speed and the nose of the plane at a proper upward angle.

During this intense training time, Richard still found time to enhance his romantic efforts with the captivating Druwanda. The $72 paycheck he received from the paymaster at the end of the month often left him short of cash for his weekend trips back to Pensacola to see Druwanda, but he was determined. He often had to borrow

$5 from other cadets so he could purchase fuel for his 1950 Pontiac Coupe. However, it came at a price. He had to repay the cadet who loaned him the money $6—a 20 percent interest charge.

One of the few times Richard became furious with a fellow cadet occurred during the training period at Bearon Field. In addition to the primary focus of the field carrier landing practice, they continued to practice aviator skills previously learned. Early one afternoon while doing formation flying, a cadet coming in from the left to join him next to his wing tip overaccelerated. Richard had to take immediate evasive actions to avoid a midair collision. Later, when everyone had landed safely and had taxied their planes to their respective hangars, he went looking for the cadet who had almost cost them their lives.

"Hey, Cadet! What the hell where you trying to pull? You almost cost us our lives!"

The young cadet stood silently, red-faced.

"Well, what do you have to say for yourself?"

Still no response, no apology, no anything.

Frustrated as hell, Richard turned and left the area. On a brighter note, he was excited when he learned gunnery practice would be incorporated into their training regimen. A huge caliber machine gun had been mounted on the front of a number of the planes. Shooting these machine guns from the plane amounted to shooting at a long wind sock being pulled from the side by another plane flying ahead of the gunnery plane.

Two major problems developed with this particular machine gun. The number 1 problem was keeping the shooting of the bullets in sync with the rotation of the propeller blade. The gun was pro-grammed to rapid fire its bullets between the propeller blades as it rotated. When it wasn't in sync, which occurred often, bullets would pierce the blades, leaving noticeable holes.

The other problem was this particular type of machine gun kept jamming. When either of these problems happened, it took sev-eral hours to rectify. Unfortunately for Richard, each time he was scheduled for gunnery practice, one of these two problems kept him from shooting practice. He was still able to fly one of the planes that had bullet holes in its propeller. He marveled at the whistling noise caused by the wind rushing through the bullet holes in the propeller.

Another tragedy occurred shortly before the conclusion of this three-month aviator training period. A cadet returning from his practice flying run encountered serious engine failure and had no choice but to abandon plane and parachute. Sadly, his chute failed to open, and he plunged to his death. Inspection of the unopened chute pack revealed that it had been incorrectly folded and packed.

The last step in achieving his wings would be training in a multi-engine plane. He couldn't wait!

25

FORREST SHERMAN FIELD

The last week at Bearon Field before transferring to Forrest Sherman Field near Pensacola was a busy time for Richard. Besides preparing for his final solo flight, he had been dealing for a brand-new car—a 1957 green Chevrolet 150. It was a six-speed stick shift and was the basic model. It had no air conditioning or a radio. The cash price for this model was $1,800. He had advertised his 1950 Pontiac Coupe in the base newspaper for $300 or best offer. He wound up selling it to another cadet for $200. With eighteen crisp one-hundred-dollar bills in hand, Richard marched into the car dealership located near the base and counted out the money to the car dealer. He was eager to give the car its first test run as the speedometer indicated the top speed was 113 mph.

After reporting in at Forrest Sherman Field, Richard made a quick visit to see Druwanda at her home, and then he headed out for a seven-day leave of absence to visit his parents in Washington, DC. Because it was a long trip, he spent the first night in Athens, Georgia, before proceeding to DC. While visiting his parents, he began to feel strangely ill. When his leave time was almost up, he decided to get a quick checkup at Bethesda Naval Hospital before heading back to Pensacola. As he sat in the waiting room before being called in, he began to worry if something wrong were discovered, he might get mustered out of the navy. He finally convinced himself that the best course of action was to leave and continue his journey back to Florida.

By the time he pulled into Athens for his overnight stay, he was feeling poorly, and his fever appeared to be high. He had no appetite, so he undressed and poured himself into bed. The bedside alarm clock rang for several seconds before he stirred. It was very difficult opening his eyelids. He felt very stiff, almost like rigor mortis had set in, and his face felt glowingly hot. With extreme difficulty, he managed to roll onto his side and work his way to the edge of the bed. Several minutes passed before he accomplished the task of getting dressed. The rest of the trip from Athens to Pensacola was a complete blur. Somehow, he was able to pull up in front of Druwanda's home. He was so exhausted it took an extra effort to press the car's horn.

Hearing the prolonged honking noise prompted Druwanda to hurry out of the house to see what was going on. As soon as she spotted Richard's car, she hurried to the driver's side. Glancing at him through the car's window, she knew something was wrong. She jerked the door open.

"Richard, Richard, honey, what's the matter?"

"I, I don't feel so hot!"

"Oh my God, you're burning up!" she declared as she felt his sweating forehead. "Move over! I'm driving you to the base hospital!" In a matter of minutes, she was helping him into the emergency room.

The doctor took one look at Richard's face and said, "Oh my God, Cadet, you've got German measles! Nurse, take this young man to the isolation ward, stat! And, missy, you go to the restroom and wash your hands and arms thoroughly with soap and warm water. When you're finished, I'll have my assistant give you a preventive shot. We don't want you to come down with the same thing!"

"Okay," she replied with a worried look on her face.

After two weeks week of being bedridden, Richard was dismissed with a clean bill of health. The downside to this confinement was that he had to work as an orderly with ward cleanup duty for two weeks. The hospital had a policy that required one cleanup day for every day one was hospitalized. Richard was highly distressed during this time. He worried and fretted that he definitely would be kicked out of the navy. But Druwanda's dad came to the rescue. He notified the base as soon as Richard was hospitalized. Her dad was a drill instructor on the base, and he had no problem getting the information to the proper authorities.

Richard's outstanding grades and class rank were his saving grace. Because of the month's setback dealing with his health issues, he also had another two to three weeks' delay before he was able to join the time frame for the next class.

Finally, in May of '57, he was assigned to begin flying the SNB-5 multi-engine plane. Its sister plane, the JRB, had no brakes on the right side of the cockpit. The copilot could work rudders on that side, but the brakes had to be worked on the pilot's side.

Richard's roommate during this training cycle was William Wright, who was 6'4". The interesting thing when they flew was the fact that William had to toss the seat cushions on his side of the plane in the rear so he could barely manage to have room to operate the rudders and brakes.

They had to each take their initial flight with an accomplished instructor. Once they were familiar with the workings of the multi-engine plane, they were then assigned to fly together.

The biggest challenge of flying the multi-engine plane was learning how to read and operate the radio instruments. When the plane flew over the ground station, a beacon would be transmitted that the radio instruments would detect. A three-letter coded signal would indicate the air base. For example, *NAS* stood for "Pensacola Naval Air Station" and *NIP* for "Jacksonville."

The final solo flight was very similar to the others Richard had undertaken. The only difference was this time it was in a multi-engine plane with a copilot.

26

DRAMATIC FINISH AT FORREST SHERMAN FIELD

The final days of the multi-engine training cycle were intense, exciting, and challenging. First and foremost on Richard's mind was his developing relationship with Druwanda. They had discussed getting engaged and then getting married following her high school graduation. When they went walking past Nickelson's Jewelry Store, they would often stop and admire the engagement/wedding rings that were displayed in the viewing window. Druwanda was quite fond of a stunning single set diamond ring, especially when the sun reflected its brilliance.

Early one afternoon before he visited with Druwanda, he stopped by the jewelry store and made arrangements to purchase the ring that Druwanda was enamored with. He would pay $20 monthly for a period of twenty-four months. Before he officially asked Druwanda to marry him, he purchased a very nice Hallmark card. In this card, he wrote for her parents' permission for Druwanda's hand in marriage.

Even though Druwanda was only seventeen years old, she knew her parents would eagerly agree to Richard's request for her hand in marriage. After all, her mother was married at the age of sixteen. Presenting the ring to Druwanda was almost anticlimactic. She and her parents were aware that he would be popping the big question to her very soon. The big excitement and thrill of this occasion was seeing her eyes and her reaction to seeing the big diamond ring of her dreams.

In the latter part of this training session, a surprise twist occurred when Richard received a phone call from a Marine Major at Sauffley Field, which was located four miles northwest of Pensacola.

"Lieutenant Warner, I'd like you to come and visit with me at 0800 hours tomorrow."

Out of curiosity he agreed.

At the appointed time the next morning, Richard knocked on the major's office door.

"Come on in, young man!"

"Yes, sir! Second Lieutenant Richard Warner reporting as requested, sir!"

"At ease, Lieutenant. Have a seat. I'll get right to the point. The Marine Corps is very impressed with your credentials. You're an accomplished pilot who ranks in the top of his class. You know our motto? We're always looking for a few good men. And you're one of them."

"What kind of flying would I do for the marines, sir?"

"We would train you to fly helicopters."

"And where does this training occur?"

"Why, right here in the Pensacola area."

Bingo, this was music to his ears! He would now be able to stay close to his fiancée, Druwanda instead of having to reporting to Hutchinson, Kansas. However, he informed the major that he still had to fly the cross-country trip in the multi-engine plane.

"No problem, Lieutenant, check in with me when you have completed this training."

"Thank you, sir!"

The exciting conclusion was to finally be awarded the naval Wings of Gold (Naval Aviation Wings). The highlight of this ceremony was that his new fiancée would get to pin his wings on him as she did his second lieutenant bars. He was very disappointed that the entire affair only lasted six to seven minutes, whereas he was expecting an elaborate ceremony with all the bells and whistles.

Before reporting to Ellison Field for his helicopter training, Richard had to successfully complete the cross-country training flight. The first leg of the cross-country flight was from Pensacola to

Chicago. This would be an overnight stop. He left in the multi-engine plane with seventy-eight gallons of fuel in each of two tanks—one located in each wing and a twenty-five-gallon tank in the nose of the plane. As he and his evaluator instructor neared the first check-in point close to their first landing stop in Chicago, he was aware, after glancing at the fuel gauge, that he needed to flip the switch to change fuel tanks. However, he was a few seconds too late and the engines quit. After fumbling around a few seconds, he was able to restart the engines. This brief error caused him to overshoot the first check-in point. The Tower advised him of his situation and guided him to a safe landing. Part of the problem was his flight instructor/evaluator failed to alert him at the critical time. He admonished Richard for his slight error in judgement. He could have actually lost his wings for this incident, but fortunately he only received a reprimand. He secretly felt his flight instructor had fallen asleep.

The second leg of the journey was an overnight stop in Denver and then on to an overnight stop at March AFB in California. The return home began with a refueling stop in Abilene, Texas, and finally back to Pensacola. The cross-country flight went well except for the incident in Chicago.

27

Ellyson Field

Richard felt a nervous excitement overcome him as he met his helicopter flight instructor for the first time. It was a hot summer day, and he was astonished to see that his flight instructor was obviously overweight and sweating profusely. After brief introductions the instructor led him to a HTL-5 Bell helicopter that was tethered nearby. Once they inspected the helicopter, they boarded it and prepared for takeoff.

"All set, Second Lieutenant Warner?"

"Yes, sir! Let's do it!"

"Here we go!"

Nothing happened. Regardless how hard he tried, the instructor could barely get the helicopter to hover a few feet above the ground. Two problems existed: one, the combined weights of the overweight instructor and Richard exceeded the maximum weight capacity of the helicopter, and two, during very hot summer days, the air becomes thin, causing a problem for the rotor blades to be able to get the lift necessary to climb. A red-faced instructor then requested for another flight instructor to take him up for his first flight.

Richard had no problem adapting to using the stick to fly the helicopter. And now that he had his officer commission and his wings, he was assigned to his own room in the living quarters. Finally, he had no roomie to contend with.

During his time at Ellyson Field, he had a two-track mind—flying the helicopter, which he excelled at, and Druwanda, whom he was madly in love with. It didn't take him long to devise a devious plan for sneaking her into his room at night. Fortunately, he was never caught. If he would have been caught in his room with Druwanda, he could have lost his wings and been kicked out of the military.

It didn't take long for Richard to transition from the HTL-5 helicopter to the HUP, a twin rotor aircraft. This helicopter's primary function was a rescue mission. It would pick up downed pilots or other military personnel who were in a distressful situation.

The number 2 seemed to be the number Richard needed to avoid. First off, in his nonscheduled time, he had agreed to fly a crew chief who needed to complete four hours of flight time.

"Lieutenant Warner?"

"Yes, what can I do for you?"

"You need to report, stat, to the major's office!"

Knock. Knock.

"Come in! We need to talk, Lieutenant Warner!"

"Yes, sir!"

"According to your log record here, you have flown one of the crew chiefs on an unauthorized mission!"

"Yes, sir, but, sir, he needed—"

"That's beside the point, young man! You are still in training, and even though you are now an officer, you are still classified as a student aviator!"

"Yes, sir!"

"I'm going to let you off on this infraction because of your outstanding performances. However, I don't want to see you in my office again!"

"Yes, sir! Thank you, sir!"

"Dismissed!"

Secondly, after achieving the status of a qualified HUP twin rotor pilot, Richard was able to schedule his flight with the scheduling officer. So in order to prolong the training and be able to spend more time with his beloved Druwanda, he procrastinated as long as he could. When checking in to schedule a flight, he would very politely give the scheduling officer permission to replace him with a pilot who desperately needed to get in some flying time.

However, after a few weeks, he was caught once again. The major wasn't thrilled to see him again in his office, but once again Richard's grades and excellent performances saved him.

"Lieutenant Warner, we're going to double up on your necessary flights, and then you'll be off to New River, North Carolina."

"Yes, sir!"

The good news was that he was going to be able to spend some time with his parents before Thanksgiving in Williamsburg, Virginia.

28

New River, North Carolina/Wedding Bells

After reporting in at New River, North Carolina, in November 1957, Richard was assigned to the HMR-261 Squadron. He was a copilot on the HUS single rotor helicopter. This chopper had a 1,500 mph engine, and its fuel tanks were rubber lined in order to avoid unexpected explosions. The primary purpose of this aircraft was to ferry men and supplies to and from offshore aircraft carriers. In addition, he was named the navigation officer for the squadron. Posting assigned squadron flight schedules, gathering and updating map data, and keeping necessary correspondence flowing in the proper channels were among his many duties.

His newly assigned duties kept Richard busy and on task because his longing for his fiancée, Druwanda, was driving him crazy. Around the first of June 1958, he informed his commanding officer of his intention of marrying his fiancée on Flag Day, June 14.

"Well, Private Lieutenant Warner, you may have Friday, June 13, to Sunday, June 15, off. Report back here at 0800 hours on Monday, June 16."

"Yes, sir! Thank you, sir!"

Even though he was hoping for at least a week off, this was better than nothing—because now he would have his beloved Druwanda by his side!

The wedding had already been preplanned and took place at 2:00 p.m. on Saturday, June 14, at East Hill Baptist Church in Pensacola, Florida.

Richard and his best man were decked out in the marine corps dress white uniform, and Druwanda was radiant in her flowing white wedding dress. She had three bridesmaids in attendance, whereas Richard had only his best man.

Rex Abercombrie, the six-year-old ring bearer, was dazzling in his miniature white officer's dress uniform.

Richard was surprised and amazed that a lieutenant commander from the navy whom he was acquainted with was in attendance at their wedding.

Although he missed out on the pomp and circumstance he had hoped for following his aviator wing ceremony, he wasn't about to let it happen during their wedding ceremony. He had solicited for and had obtained permission for a six-man marine corps honor guard to participate in their wedding ceremony.

After the exchange of their wedding nuptials and the exchange of wedding rings at the front of the church, the wedding party prepared to exit down the aisle through the marine corps honor guard. Three marines faced three other marines on either side of the aisle near the front of the church. When the pastor gave his nod to the organist to begin playing the wedding recessional song, he then motioned for the wedding party to leave.

At the appointed time the marine sergeant who headed the honor guard called them to attention.

"Detail! Ten-hut! Order, arms!"

At this command, the detail brought their swords to vertical attention in front of their faces.

"Detail! Present, arms!"

At this time, the marines extended their swords point to point at approximately a thirty-degree angle in front of them.

Rex Abercrombie, the ring bearer, began the exit procession. He was followed by the three bridesmaids and then the best man. With Druwanda's left hand firmly clasped in his right hand, Richard proudly escorted his new bride ahead of him through the marine corps honor guard.

A huge wedding reception was held at a nearby country club. Over three hundred guests were present to help celebrate the occasion. Druwanda's family members and close friends later gathered up over three hundred wedding presents and stowed them at Druwanda's parents' house.

At the conclusion of the wedding reception, Richard had his best man deliver him and Druwanda to her home. There they quickly changed from their wedding attire to casual dress. Their honeymoon was going to be a short trip back to New River, North Carolina.

Grabbing their suitcases, they hurried from the house to the unattached garage. After he lifted the garage door open, Druwanda let out a huge gasp.

"What the!" She stared in disbelief at the sight of his 1957 Chevrolet in front of her. The car sat there sparkling clean, ready for departure.

"What's the matter, dear?" Richard inquired of his new bride.

Druwanda stalked around the car.

"Where are the 'Just Married' shaving cream letters on the sides of the car? Where are the tied-up tin cans that should be trailing behind the bumper? And where are the streamers that should be tied to the radio antenna?"

Richard was at a loss for words. He had secretly hired some neighborhood teenagers he was well acquainted with to make sure no one tampered with his vehicle. He had no idea Druwanda wanted the world to be aware of their marital status. He gave several feeble attempts at an apology, but to no avail. Druwanda was steaming mad. She sat with her arms folded across her chest and stared out the window when they departed.

However, as they left the Pensacola area, she slowly edged her way to his side, especially when he started to hum their favorite song. Before long she was snuggled next to him, saying sweet nothings in his ear. Needless to say, keeping the car on the road was a difficult task.

29

NEW RIVER/BACK TO REALITY

In July 1958, the HMR-261 Squadron was ordered to prepare for duty in Lebanon. Prior to the departure date, some of the big-wheel brass from Washington, DC, and the Pentagon visited the aircraft carrier, the Antietam. Richard was thrilled that a photo of this occasion was featured on the cover of *Life Magazine*. And even though he was the only one who could actually pick out his position on the photo, he was very proud of the fact that he made the cover of *Life Magazine*. Also, President Dwight D. Eisenhower visited the area during this time.

An unexpected accident occurred about this time that would leave an everlasting impression on Richard and would come to haunt his dreams years later. A pilot, Sergeant Coyadus, was assigned to assist in the loading of the aircraft carrier. Sergeant Coyadus was one of the senior pilots of the squadron, and he was also one of the last NCOs to achieve helicopter pilot status. He was a very experienced pilot whom all the squadron's pilots and copilots admired. He was extremely safety conscious, and everyone affectionately called him "Grandmother." He was assigned to pilot a H04S helicopter, which was an older version of the HUS helicopter. On this particular hot, dry morning, Sergeant Coyadus and his copilot were to ferry a passenger, First Lieutenant Ken Karsdorf, to the aircraft carrier. The incoming air traffic would approach the carrier at deck level so as to avoid outgoing air traffic. As they neared the ship's deck, Sergeant Coyadus attempted to gain the necessary lift to make it up and over the deck of the ship. However, in helicopter pilots' terminology, he lost his turn, where the copter stalls out and doesn't lift. The helicopter then lost needed power and slowly descended into the water.

"Chopper down! Chopper down!" a chorus of alarming voices shouted from the ship.

Richard, who was standing near the railing of the ship where the helicopter went down, was in disbelief and shock.

Sergeant Coyadus and his copilot were safely rescued. Unfortunately, First Lieutenant Ken Karsdorf, who was situated in the lower level of the helicopter, drowned before he was able to be safely rescued. A portable crane was brought in to aid in the rescue with the help of several navy frogmen. They were finally able to free the lieutenant from the helicopter and lift him aboard the aircraft carrier.

The image of the dead lieutenant being hoisted from the water in a sitting position, with his right arm and hand stretched upward as if trying to grab on to something, would be etched into Richard's subconscious forever. The body of Lieutenant Ken Karsdorf was immediately placed in a black bag and carted away.

An investigation following the tragic accident would come to the conclusion that the accident was the result of pilot error. As a consequence, Sergeant Coyadus was demoted in rank and transferred out of the squadron. No one ever knew what happened to him after that.

30

MARRIED LIFE BEGINS

Druwanda was impressed! Due to his status as navigation officer for his squadron and his marital status, Richard was allotted housing in quarters that were for high-ranking officers. They were actually allowed to live in a house that was designated for officers with the rank of major. It was a three-bedroom house that was equipped with a fireplace and a carport. He even had his own name and rank displayed on a nameplate in front of the house, much to the dismay and envy of several of the officers in his squadron.

During this time, Richard's military duties remained basically status quo—biweekly flights to and from the aircraft carrier coupled with his duties as navigation officer for his squadron kept him busy. In the evenings and on weekends, he enjoyed the time he got to spend with his new bride, Druwanda.

They decided they wanted to start a family. And nine months later, on April 26, 1959, their first child, a boy, was born at the naval hospital in Camp Lejeune, North Carolina. They named the young lad Devin Bertwill. The unusual middle name was the combination of two of the names of the baby's uncles.

About this time, the aircraft carrier was destined to report for duty off the coast of Lebanon in the Middle East. Richard was surprised when he was summoned to appear in the lieutenant colonel's office aboard the carrier.

"First Lieutenant Warner reporting as ordered, sir!"

"At ease, Lieutenant. We've been ordered to bring a civilian tech aboard the carrier for our deployment to Lebanon. To make room for him, we have to cut one of our military personnel because we don't have additional room on the ship. So in lieu of the fact that you're a newlywed with a young son to care for, we've decided that you are the one who will be returned to shore. So pack your duffel bag and be ready to return to shore on the next shuttle flight."

"Yes, sir! Thank you, sir!"

Richard was thrilled. He would not be separated from his family! Ironically, shortly before the aircraft carrier was to depart, orders came down from the Pentagon cancelling the deployment. Instead, the carrier was diverted to performing military maneuvers in the Costa Rica area.

In February 1960 First Lieutenant Richard Warner, having completed his initial four-year commitment in the military, was given his separation papers and assigned to marine reserve status.

He and his young family settled in Pensacola, Florida, near Druwanda's parents' home. They purchased a house for $16,000 in the suburb Scenic Heights. Their house payments were $75 a month.

Richard went to work for his father-in-law's insurance agency. His father-in-law was the general agent for Volunteer State Life Insurance, which was headquartered in Tennessee. Their primary insurance products were life and health policies. The premium policy they featured was a $20,000 whole life policy. Valuewise, it was the best deal they had to offer. His starting salary was $400 a month. His initial first three months on the job was a total bust—not one sale was generated! About this time, he was ready to quit and search for another job. But with his father-in-law's encouragement, he finally made his first sale.

The basic sales technique Richard employed was to scan the daily newspaper for recent birth announcements. He would then call on the young family to present his sale pitch. If he was unsuccessful at achieving a sale, he would politely ask for possible referrals.

Richard's diligence and outstanding work ethic paid off. In less than a year during one-month's period of time, he achieved the rank of fourth in sales for the entire company. During this time, he was also elected secretary for the local Life Underwriters' Association. His almost crowning achievement was barely missing the $1,000,000 Life Sales Round Table for the company in 1961.

In August of 1962 (although not unexpected), Richard was recalled into active duty status at Camp Lejeune, North Carolina. On December 28, 1962, their daughter Daree was born. Her unusual name was also the result of a combination of a couple of names.

31

BACK TO NEW RIVER

With a young family to support Richard decided to drive a VW Bug while selling insurance in the Pensacola and surrounding areas. He was always in a hurry, and he became somewhat impatient with the Bug because he could only get a top speed of 68 mph out of it—unless it was aided by a strong tailwind, then it might reach 72 mph. But hey, it was very economical to run, and it was very maneuverable in tight spaces.

A telephone call in August 1962 would change the comfortable life style he and his family were accustomed to.

"Hello, this is Richard Warner."

"Richard Warner, captain in the marine reserves?"

"Yes, sir!"

"I have been empowered to inform you to report for active duty in two weeks to your former squadron in New River, North Carolina. You have this time to get your affairs in order."

"Yes, sir!"

During his reserve military status, Richard had been promoted to the rank of captain. From the rumors that circulated in the reserve establishment, the call that he received wasn't unexpected—although somewhat dreaded.

Richard and Druwanda sold their house, and he traded his VW Bug in for a green 1960 two-door Chevy Bel-Air.

After the move back to New River, he was assigned as a squadron pilot in his old unit. In addition, he was also promoted to division commander. Several of the officers in his squadron with a rank of captain had logged several more flying hours than he had. Instead of lording his division commander's position over them, he utilized their flying experiences to his advantage. He often called for their advice regarding a particular mission, and he would give them seniority in strategic situations.

Two worrisome hot spots loomed on the horizon—racial tension in Mississippi and the Cuban Missile Crisis. In a matter of weeks in September 1962, the entire Marine Air Group (MAG), under the leadership of Colonel Keith B. McCutcheon, was sent to Meridian, Mississippi.

During the early '60s, racial unrest was rampant in the country, most notably in the South. Many black people were vocally and physically protesting their rights for equal education, transportation, jobs, etc. A particular hot spot was Oxford, Mississippi, where a young black man, James Meredith, was attempting to enroll at Ole Miss University.

Richard's squadron would fly recon missions to Oxford from Meridian for a week. After Mr. Meredith was successfully enrolled in Ole Miss under careful supervision, the marine air group was ordered to return to New River.

Following this crisis, the Cuban Missile Crisis reared its ugly head. Some of the marine air group was sent to southern Florida during this time when the mounting tensions between the Soviet Union and the United States flared up. The time span for this confrontation was October to November 1962.

After things began to quiet down, Richard enrolled in a supply course held at Montford Point. This was a very demanding, intense course crammed into a time frame of one month. Because he ranked seventh in his class, he was awarded an all-purpose supply officer position. His numerical status was 3002, which entitled him to be placed in any supply area in the corps.

In a matter of days, he was assigned as base supply officer to Camp Lejeune, which was located across the river from New River. His position was impressive, as he had command control over twenty-six officers who were primarily privates and second lieutenants. Among the officers, he was in charge with was First Lieutenant

Charles Robb, who would later marry one of President Lyndon Johnson's daughters. He would later be elected a senator from the State of Virginia.

Even though Richard's new duties kept him quite busy, he still enjoyed his evenings and weekends with his young family. One of his fond memories was recalling the wide-eyed expression on his son Devin's face when he presented him with his first toy, a red monkey that he had purchased on a training mission to Texas. Devin loved sucking on the monkey's feet.

Also during this time, Richard and Druwanda enrolled in a Russian language class together. Druwanda was a bright student and was a step ahead of him in the class, partially due to the fact he wasn't able to attend all the sessions because of his military obligations. They were secretly hoping to eventually secure translator positions at the US Embassy in the Soviet Union. Richard's high energy level compelled him to also enroll in a course involving masonry. He had become interested in masonry work growing up in DC when he would help his dad and uncle.

However, all this extra activity was cut short in May 1965.

"Captain Warner, here are your orders to report to Okinawa."

"What! Are you kidding me?"

"No, Captain, I'm not. You have a week to make arrangements for your family."

"But, but, sir! I have two young children!"

"I'm aware of your family situation, Captain. But orders are orders, and we all must serve when and where we are needed. And they need a supply officer of your caliber in Okinawa."

"Yes, sir!"

"Dismissed, Captain!"

32

ORDERED TO OKINAWA

Druwanda was equally as shocked and dismayed with the deployment order her husband had received. To help alleviate the family burden, which now fell on her shoulders, they rented a house near her parents in Pensacola, Florida. She would at least have her parents nearby when she needed help.

Richard was appointed the supply officer for the Third Marine Tank Battalion, which was located at a new marine base called Camp Hansen. The marines either fondly or not so fondly referred to Okinawa as Oki-knock-knock.

A warrant officer by the name of Norm Goodwin, who was the battalion chaplain, was also assigned to Richard's supply detail, along with fourteen sergeants, corporals, and privates. Warrant Officer Goodwin had enlisted in the British Navy and later transferred to the marine corps on the East Coast of the United States. Their friendship solidified when they discovered they had a mutual religious affiliation with the Seventh-day Adventist Church. The headquarters for the Seventh-day Adventist Church was located in Tacoma Park, Maryland. Richard's mother had strong ties with the church.

He further enhanced his ties with Chaplin Goodwin thanks to his knowledge of the precepts and tenets of the Seventh-day Adventist Church. When he made arrangements for meals for his supply crew, he made sure no meat was in the chaplain's meals.

The separation from Druwanda and his children was increasingly difficult for Richard. Almost daily he would write her a long and endearing letter. Although he looked forward to receiving letters from her, they only seemed to compound his misery from missing her so much. Thank God he did get to hear her voice once or twice a week via a ham radio operator. The difficulty in these conversations with her was the protocol they had to follow, for example:

"Hi, Druwanda, over."

"Hi, Richard, over."

"I miss you, honey, over."

"I miss you too, over."

"How are the kids, over."

"They're fine, over."

Richard learned to proofread his letters before sending them to Druwanda because he would often spot an "over" at the end of a sentence.

To occupy his downtime in Okinawa, Richard enrolled in a correspondence accounting course from the University of Maryland. He wasn't actually sure how he was going to utilize the knowledge from this course, but it kept him mentally occupied.

This overseas deployment also introduced him to cultural shock. The physical labor for the various marine base construction projects, including the base chapel, was supplied by the women from the local villages. The men stood around in hard hats and were the designated supervisors.

A month later in June1965, the entire Third Marine Tank Battalion was given orders to set sail for Vietnam in July. Vietnam was becoming an increasing hot spot for military action. The collective response of most of the marines was, "Oh s———!"

Neither Richard nor Druwanda was thrilled with the news.

33

VIETNAM? OH S——!

Lieutenant Colonel S. R. Jones personally told Captain Warner of the impending deployment to Vietnam in June. After recovering from the shock of the news, Richard got his thinking cap on and began preparing for the move to an even hotter climate in Vietnam. After gathering his supply NCOs together he informed them of the move and the weather conditions they would be dealing with. He instructed them to scavenge all the usable refrigerator and air conditioning parts they could find at the local marine base dumping grounds. He was proud of these creative NCOs, who would do miraculous things with these usable parts once they arrived in Vietnam.

In late July, they shipped out for Vietnam on a LST flat-bottom boat with the numerical designation of 1166. This boast was designed to haul and deliver tanks ashore on the landing beach. These flat-bottom boats appeared to be a little unstable in rough waters.

In a few days, they were deposited on the northeast shore of Vietnam near Da Nang. They were located at I Corps Marine Base near an air force base. They were able to walk ashore from the LST landing ship because it was designated an administrative landing zone.

Richard was surprised. It seemed that all the military factions had their designated protected areas. The air force personnel to their right enjoyed uninterrupted swimming and beach privileges, as did their enemy, the Viet Cong, on their left side. It was as if they were daring each other to cross the line.

Captain Richard Warner's commanding officer was impressed with his leadership skills and creative abilities to get things done.

He informed Richard of his intent to groom him for a personal aide position with a general. This was welcome news for Richard as it would enable him to end his military career on a high note in an enviable position. This would guarantee him an eventual promotion to a full bird colonel.

Unfortunately, in the days that followed, Richard began to become unnerved by the constant shelling in the nearby distance. That coupled with the continual flow of incoming KIAs (killed in action) was too much for him to handle.

They had only been in country about a month when Richard sought the advice and counsel of the base psychologist.

"Come in, Captain Warner! Please have a seat. How can I help you?"

"Well, sir, I'm kind of embarrassed to admit it, but I'm scared of being here in Nam."

"What is it that seems to be scaring you?"

"Well, sir, the constant shelling, especially at night, and seeing all of those KIAs coming in daily really bother me."

"I understand your feelings, Captain, but most of us here in Nam are going through the same thing—including me."

"You too, sir?"

"Yes, me too. But you'll learn to deal with it—most of the rest of us have."

"Okay, thank you, sir."

"You're welcome, Captain."

In subsequent meetings with his commanding officer, Richard's answers to the commander's questions seemed to be all over the place.

"Captain Warner, you know what?"

"What's that, sir?"

"You're like a damn bunny rabbit! Your answers are all over the place!"

"Yes, sir, but—"

"No buts, Captain! Dismissed. Tell you what, go to the officer's club and have a drink!"

The "bunny rabbit" tag would stay with Richard forever.

34

SLIDING IN S——!

An enjoyable evening at the marine officer's club one evening was suddenly interrupted by a loud thump on Richard's back.

"Well, lookie who we have here. Why, it's Captain Richard Warner! Aren't you out of uniform, Captain?"

"Huh, what? Why, it's Captain Ray Root!"

"Front and center, Captain Warner!"

"What are you doing here?"

"Just delivering supplies, as usual."

One of the officers at the table inquired of Captain Root, "What did you mean by Captain Warner here being out of uniform?"

"That's an interesting story, isn't it, Captain Warner!" He laughed as he slapped Richard on his shoulder.

"I'll tell you what, buy me a drink and I'll fill you in on the details!"

"That's a deal!" they shouted out.

"The good captain and I were training at Bogue Field off the coast of North Carolina doing maneuvers. We were flying an HUS helicopter. Our assignment was to ferry cans of H2O from the aircraft carrier situated off Onslow Beach to Cherry Point, where a camp was being set up. We were on a tight schedule, and as soon as we unloaded our supplies, we had to head back to the carrier for another load.

"Well, as we unloaded our second drop, Captain Warner informed me of his urgent need to take a 'load off of his mind'—if you know what I mean! So I told him to hurry and get it over with.

Captain Warner asked the sergeant receiving the supplies where the latrine was located. The good Sergeant told him to just follow the path and he couldn't miss it.

"The desperate captain here went running up the path, which meandered over a slight incline. Well, about three hundred yards up the path, he was confronted by a huge log lying across the path. Our quick-thinking captain decided in a split second to hurdle the log. His right heel hit a gooey mess, and his legs went out from under him, and he went sliding in a stinking pile of marine s——! According to our man here, after he had shouted several expletives, he then tried rolling in the nearby grassy area to rid him of the filthy excrement.

"The irony of this hilarious situation is that the marines who needed to do their duty would drop their drawers, extend their posteriors over the edge of the log, and do their thing. A roll of toilet paper was tucked near the end of the log on the other side.

"Anyways, after several minutes, Captain Warner returned to the chopper. When I saw this smelly s—— covered creature, I refused to let him aboard. I demanded he take off his uniform and leave it in a pile. Red-faced and muttering expletives, he climbed on board in his white T-shirt and boxers. I returned him to Bogue Field. Obviously, he headed to his barracks under the curious stare of several of his fellow marines!"

The officers at the table gave Captain Root a standing ovation amid shouts of "Semper Fi! Semper Fi!" much to the chagrin of a red-faced captain.

35

GOING HOME!

The constant shelling by the Viet Cong, coupled with incidents of Viet Cong soldiers attempting to penetrate the base's perimeter, continued to dominate Richard's dreams. He became sleep deprived because of these fears that haunted him. The Viet Cong had a reputation for their tenacious suicidal behavior. They might send a young lad with a hand grenade into their midst or decapitate you with a piano wire when you were unaware or asleep.

So Richard's paranoid response to his demons was to lie in bed with a loaded .45 pistol on his chest. This was his teddy bear.

Visits with the base chaplain gave him some comfort as the chaplain seemed to understand his personal crisis. Finally, after several visits, the chaplain had to inform Richard:

"Captain Warner."

"Yes, Chaplain?"

"I've concurred with your company commander, and we believe our best course of action regarding your situation is to send you to sick bay at the field hospital."

"Do you think that's necessary?"

"We do. Some of your men have noticed tears streaming down your cheeks when you address them. So we're hoping with some rest and medication to reduce your anxiety levels, you'll be able to return to your duties."

"Thank you, sir!"

"I'm praying for your recovery, Captain."

Unfortunately, Richard's mental and emotional status didn't improve. His company commander felt compelled to write orders transferring him back to a hospital in the States.

After the transfer orders were issued, Captain Warner was ushered aboard a Medevac plane that was utilized primarily to transport the critically wounded Stateside. A limited nursing staff was kept quite busy trying to minister to their injured patients. Richard sat isolated in a seat near the front of the plane. Every hour an air force nurse would give him a blue pill to take.

Their first stop was an overnight stay at Tripler Army Hospital in Hawaii. Richard was placed in a restrictive mental ward of the hospital. He was confused as he wasn't even allowed to use a razor. The 40 mg of medication they gave him every half hour had a reverse effect on how he felt; he seemed more perplexed and in a dazed state.

The next stop on their way home was an overnight stop at Fort Sam Houston in San Antonio, Texas. The personnel at the hospital made Richard feel more at ease. They were very polite and considerate, and, he didn't recall getting pumped with a bunch of pills.

Finally, the last leg of the journey was underway to the naval hospital located in Philadelphia, Pennsylvania. Unfortunately, on the way to Philly, Captain Warner threw up in the aisle of the plane. The vomit was riddled with twenty-plus blue pill containers—some open, some intact. A medic who was on the plane informed Richard that he believed he was overdosed with this potent medication.

After he was made comfortable in the mental ward at the hospital in Philly, he called Druwanda in Pensacola and asked her to send him some of his uniforms. However, she was in shock by the request, and Richard had to put a doctor on the line to verify his request. He had left Vietnam without any of his personal belongings.

After a month of intense observations and evaluations, a panel of five medical officers came to the conclusion that Captain Richard Warner was suffering from pseudo schizophrenia. They prescribed valium to help him deal with his mental problems. The Warner's phone bill during this time was a whopping $200!

Captain Warner was issued a temporary disability retirement order and told to meet with a designated navy psychiatrist in the Pensacola area.

Druwanda showed up in a frugal Nash Rambler to take her recovering husband home.

36

BACK TO SQUARE ONE

In addition to meeting with the navy psychiatrist once a month, Richard accepted a temporary position with Sears and Roebuck during the Christmas season. He was assigned to the housewares division of the store. He was thrilled to be back at work again. His only complaint was working with Gladys Pederson, who headed the housewares division. She was very bossy and liked everyone to know it. It didn't take long for Richard's outstanding work ethic to be noticed. Bill Gill, a retired army bomber pilot from World War II, was impressed with his attention to detail and his relationships with the customers. Bill headed Division 46-47, which was the appliance division, consisting of air conditioning units, refrigerators, stoves, etc.

"Did you want to see me, sir?"

"Yes, Mr. Warner. Please have a seat. I'm very impressed with your dedication to Sears and Roebuck. I would like to offer you a salesman position in my appliance division. The leadership skills you exhibited in your military career make you an ideal candidate for us. Your basically impeccable resume attests to this."

"It sounds interesting, sir. What does the position entail?"

"You will be operating on our main floor helping sell our top line of appliances. You will be sort of an apprentice the first couple of weeks so you can become familiar with our products. And during this time, you will be able to observe the selling techniques of our established sales personnel."

"Sounds good to me. What's your pay scale?"

"We'll give you a monetary draw to cover your first few weeks on the job. After that you'll be on a 100 percent commission basis. And with your personality and work ethic, you'll do very well."

"Okay, it's a deal. When do I start?"

Within months, Richard was the top performing salesman for the division. However, during a three-month period he failed to meet his sales quota, and as a consequence he had to accept a commission's draw to make up the difference, which he had no problem in repaying in the succeeding months.

Because he was a retired veteran, an acquaintance of his encouraged him to take the civil service test in order to land a government job. After twenty-two months of employment at Sears and Roebuck from December 1965 to October 1967, he resigned and took a civil service position at a nearby naval air rework facility.

This facility was an overhaul department point for naval aircraft. Richard was given an apprenticeship in an instrument shop. The employees in the shop had to bathe before entering, wear a white uniform and cap, and rubber treated gloves. Once they were situated at their working benches, the entire area was vacuumed to eliminate all dust particles. Each worker wore an eye magnifying glass in order to perform their intricate tasks. They had to oil small bearings to rid them of imperfections. These bearings were used in the instrumental panels of the aircraft.

After five months in this tedious position, Richard applied for and was granted an entry-level job as a management analyst. His designation was in the 343-GS5 series. He had to attend classroom sessions to become a "time and study man." This entailed efficiency measurement of personnel.

At the GS7 level, he was involved in setting methods of standards and performances in the various work areas.

A few years later, when he achieved the GS9 level, his duties included looking at written reports on a weekly basis to determine if performance standards were being met.

On a yearly basis, Richard would apply for promotion to the GS11 level, to no avail, even though he was number 1 on the list to be recognized. Ironically a letter he had written to the authorities that exposed corruption within the system probably secured the promotion for him. He was called into his boss's office and told he had reached the GS1 level. He was also told that his letter would end there.

Having finally attained the GS11 level, he was sent to the base commander's office, which was located in Building 52. He was in charge of detecting problem areas and then coming up with a viable solution to them—for example, investigating and checking fuel lines in the base's fuel system.

After seventeen years in the civil service field, Richard decided to resign and seek employment elsewhere for three prime reasons: (1) at this point in time, the military began farming out jobs to civilian contractors, (2) the government union was becoming too powerful, and (3) he was actually giving up $5,000 in pay because of his military reserve status and the fact that he was a non-union member.

He was ready to move on—to see if the grass was greener on the other side of the fence.

37

WEDDING ANNIVERSARIES

For most married couples, wedding anniversaries are memorable occasions. From greeting cards that portray that special sentiment to her favorite flowers, it is a festive occasion to be celebrated. After an exchange of meaningful gifts (usually in the early twilight), an evening out at a favorite restaurant is in store. For the wife, that special gift is often some sort of jewelry, and oftentimes for the husband, some sporting goods equipment or maybe a needed tool.

Some couples like to give a gift that reflects the traditional anniversary symbol for that year—for example, for the first anniversary, paper; for the second, cotton; the third, leather; fourth, flowers; tenth, tin; twentieth, china; thirtieth, pearl, etc.

Richard recalls that on their first wedding anniversary after an exchange of cards and his presentation of a dozen red roses to Druwanda, he presented her with a paper gift in keeping with the tradition of a gift of paper. He had ordered a special box of floral stationery with her name highlighted on each page for her. Druwanda's first anniversary gift to Richard was a smoking pipe, which caught him by surprise because he didn't smoke.

Following these wedding anniversary formalities, he then took her out for dinner at one of their favorite restaurants in the Pensacola area, which was called Martines. This popular eating establishment was known for its variety of fresh fish. One of their all-time favorites was a platter featuring scamp and all the trimmings. Scamp is a protogynous grouper; it is also known as the brown or abadejo fish. This fish is a very popular game and commercial fish in the Florida area.

It is often found on reef ledges, and it is considered a very excellent eating fish.

Their drink of choice to go with the meal was a whiskey sour, and for dessert hot fudge ice cream was the favorite.

Of course, this wonderful dining experience was capped off by an intimate affair at home.

The only questionable anniversary that Richard could recall where plans went awry was their tenth anniversary. The day started off fine. After a good breakfast, he and Druwanda exchanged cards, and he presented her with ten red roses in honor of their tenth anniversary. The plans for the rest of the morning and afternoon were to have a pleasant time in the company of their two children, Devin and Daree. In the evening they would go to an upscale restaurant and enjoy a dinner and drinks. Druwanda loved ballroom dancing, and it was the featured entertainment at this place. In fact, she was a very good ballroom dancer.

But this vision of what was about to be was drastically changed by a phone call.

"Hey, Dad, the phone is for you," Devin shouted from the kitchen.

"Okay, son, I'm coming. Hello, this is Richard speaking."

"Hey, Richard, we got a good gig here at the NCO Club, and we could sure use you to help the band out by playing drums for us."

"Well, I don't know, this is our tenth anniversary today, and we have big plans for this evening."

"I tell you what, Richard, we'll pay you ten dollars and hour for a six-hour gig—that's sixty dollars! And we will take care of the snacks and drinks."

"Druwanda, the band needs a drummer tonight at the NCO Club. What do you think I should do?"

"Well, dear, we do have plans for this evening, but it's your choice."

"I know, sweetheart, but they will pay me sixty dollars, and you know we could sure use the money."

"We do need the money. Go ahead and do what you want to do."

"Thanks!" Back to the phone, "I guess I'll take the gig."

"Great! See you at seven."

Years later, Richard would reflect back on this anniversary and ponder whether or not he had made the right choice.

38

FAMILY LIFE IN THE
'70S AND '80S

When Devin and Daree were youngsters, Richard and Druwanda would often take them to a children's Sunday school service at Warrington Baptist Church. Their children thoroughly enjoyed this time intermingling with the other children and learning about their Christian faith. During this time, Richard would often take Druwanda to a nearby Howard Johnson's for breakfast. This gave them some alone time, which they savored. After one such outing, Richard was accosted by the pastor when he returned to pick up the children. He accused Richard and his wife of using the church for a babysitting service. This prompted them to take up membership at the First Baptist Church, which was in their neighborhood.

In addition, Richard and his wife continued with a practice they had actually begun when they were first dating. They relished attending a movie together on a weekly basis whenever possible. Their willing babysitters were usually Druwanda's parents.

These early growing-up years with his children produced some memorable moments for Richard.

When Devin was quite young, he took him to a boxing match. Once the match had commenced and the boxers started to exchange blows, Devin grabbed his dad's arm, and with eyes wide open and staring, he wanted to know why they were hurting each other. Realizing he had made a mistake, Richard left the boxing match with his son and treated him to an ice cream cone at an ice cream store.

Another memorable moment was when he took Devin on his first fishing trip. And although they only caught one fish, a blowfish, Devin was excited. After they returned home with their prize catch, they went to a supply store and purchased a large glass jar and some formaldehyde. The following Monday at school, Devin proudly displayed his blowfish to the class.

A few years later, when their daughter Daree started kindergarten, she embarrassed her daddy. In an introductory session, the students were to tell the rest of the class what their fathers' jobs were. When it came for Daree's turn, she proudly stood up and proclaimed, "My daddy's a retarded marine!"

Of course, Druwanda found it to be quite amusing!

Daree had an early growing spurt, and she often had to deal with sharp pains in her knees and ankles. During this time, she also had a slight speech impediment as she mispronounced certain letters. One evening Richard noticed that Daree appeared to be having difficulty walking across the room.

"What's the matter, honey? Are your legs hurting you again?"

"Yes, Daddy, my regs are hurting me!"

After years working at his civil service job Richard had accumulated several weeks of vacation time. He set ambitious goals for this time to be with his family. He decided, with the sake of his children's education in mind, to take them on a tour of every state capital in the continental USA.

In 1976 when Devin was twelve years old and Daree was ten, they traveled the western half of the country visiting the state capitals. The following year in 1977, they toured the state capitals in the eastern half of the country. The negative feedback Richard received from his family was that too much time was spent traveling and not enough time spent enjoying the sites.

Both Devin and Daree were interested in music. Devin enjoyed playing the drums and was a drummer for a few of the local high school bands. Daree, on the other hand, was interested in singing. One of her favorite singers she tried to emulate was Olivia Newton John. Richard would often hear Daree playing her songs when he returned home from work.

Devin and Daree's musical interests and talents could obviously be traced to their mother. Druwanda was adept at playing the piano, flute, sax, and she probably could have easily played about any instrument that she would have had an interest in playing. Richard had purchased a nice Hammond organ for her, and she and the kids would often have their own jam sessions in the evening. Devin would add a background of drum beats while Daree would blare out saxophone notes to their mother's accompaniment on the organ.

Richard fondly recalled his daughter's dismay during the Christmas shopping season when she was seventeen and she and a couple of the high school band members, who were also accomplished athletes, were playing a gig at a local shopping mall. Both of the athlete/musicians were over six feet tall. Once they had their instruments in tune, one of the guys announced to the small crowd that had gathered around to listen to them that they would begin playing as soon as Daree stood up. Of course, she was already standing, and her face turned beet red while the crowd snickered in delight.

Richard's biggest concern was for Druwanda's safety during this period of time. She would occasionally take a gig playing piano for a local night club. This meant she would often return home in the wee hours of the morning. In addition to his concerns for her well-being, he had to secretly deal with his feelings of insecurity and jealousy.

Devin and Daree were also very active in their academic studies—both were straight A students. Devin excelled in US geography—the state capitals tours were probably instrumental in his achievement. In her senior year, Daree was the drum major for the high school band, as well as the editor for the school newspaper.

Daree was proud to follow in her mother's footsteps as her mother had also been a drum major, and she was happy to wear the same uniforms her mother had worn. These special outfits were made by her grandmother.

Druwanda was a model homemaker during their children's school years. She could have been an interior decorator as she kept all the rooms up to date with the current trends. In addition to being an accomplished cook, she was also an excellent seamstress. One of the first major purchases Richard had made following their wedding was to buy a first-rate Singer sewing machine.

After Devin and Daree entered their teen years, she accepted a teller position with Pen Air Federal Credit Union.

39

WESTERN HOSPITALITY ON DISPLAY

In 1970, the Warner family headed out west from Pensacola, Florida, on their summer sojourn to visit western state capitals. Richard was super excited to be taking his family on this educational sightseeing trip. And he was especially proud of the new 1970 four-door Mercury Montego that he would chauffer them around in.

After an overnight stop in Amarillo, Texas, they arrived at their first destination: Denver, Colorado. This fast-growing western city nestled at the foot of the Rocky Mountains was very picturesque. After a quick lunch, they hurried to visit the Colorado State Capitol Building, with its golden dome situated at 5,280 feet above sea level, hence the nickname of the city as the Mile-High City. They were impressed with the large legislative rotunda and the spiraling stairs to the base of the dome.

Following the tour of the state capitol building, Richard took the family to the famed Elitch amusement park, which was located at Thirty-Eighth and Tennyson Streets. This amusement park was founded on May 1, 1890, on sixteen acres of land. One of its main attractions was its luscious floral gardens, which Druwanda thoroughly enjoyed touring. Of course, their children, Devin and Daree, were thrilled with several rides on the famous premier roller coaster, the Wildcat. This sixty-eight-foot-high wooden roller coaster featured several up and downs and twists and a ride lasted one minute and forty-five seconds. This amusement park would move to its new location in downtown Denver in 1994.

Evening time was fast approaching as Richard gathered the family together to head out for their next stop, the Wyoming State Capitol located in Cheyenne, Wyoming. Even though Cheyenne was the state capital, its population in 1970 was only 41,254 residents. Unfortunately, the dozen or so motels/hotels were all booked solid. An exasperated Druwanda and the children were not too thrilled with this prospect.

"I told you it was getting late and that we should probably spend the night in Denver," she admonished Richard. It was nearing 10:00 p.m.

"Hey, everyone, let's just cool down and think this out, okay? Tell you what, Devin, you and Daree have been complaining about being hungry, so let's grab something to eat and discuss the matter. Not far from the state capitol, they located a McDonald's that was still open. Richard parked the car, and everyone went inside as they all needed to use the restroom facilities.

While their orders were being filled, he queried the evening manager whether or not if he knew of any available lodging for the evening. Charlie Gibson, the manager, named off several motels and hotels, to which Richard replied they were all full.

Feeling sorry for this seemingly distraught family, Charlie stated, "Tell you what, Richard, if you and your family can wait another hour until I close, I will have you follow me to my residence. It so happens I have a brand-new travel trailer setting in my backyard that I've never used. You're welcome to use it."

"Thank you, sir, we sure do thank you for your help."

"Glad to help out," Charlie stated.

Charlie's travel trailer was very nice and spacious. Following a relatively peaceful night's sleep, Richard and his family arose early to continue with their journey. After they were packed and ready to go, he left a brief thank-you note in the kitchen sink of the trailer along with a fifty-dollar bill to show their appreciation for the kindness Charlie had shown them.

In a few minutes after leaving Charlie's residence, they discovered a Denny's Restaurant and decided to eat breakfast there, before they began their tour of the Wyoming State Capitol Building. While they were waiting for their breakfast orders to be served, they discussed the previous day's activities, pros and cons, and what the day's agenda was going to entail. Suddenly, they were interrupted by a voice from a nearby table.

"Excuse me, family, I couldn't but help hearing your conversation. It sounds like you are on vacation from out of state. My name is Robert Younger, I own the Ford dealership here in Cheyenne. I would like to present you with four tickets to attend our featured event, the world-famous rodeo going on right now at Frontier Days."

"Wow, I don't know what to say!" a surprised Richard replied.

"You don't have to say anything. Please be my guests."

"Oh, thank you, sir, we've never been to a rodeo before!"

"You're welcome, I guarantee you will enjoy it."

"Well, guys, looks like we will be attending a rodeo today. We will tour the State Capitol tomorrow."

"Oh, thank you, Daddy," Devin and Daree chimed in.

"But we are going to secure room accommodations for the evening, first!" Druwanda cautioned.

The children especially enjoyed the thrills of the various rodeo events, from horseback riding and bull riding to steer wrestling and roping. Their only cause for alarm was when a steer roper lost his thumb trying to dislodge the rope from around the steer's horns.

Following their tour of the Wyoming State Capitol Building the next morning, Richard announced, "Montana, here we come!"

40

A New Career - Driving a Semi-Truck

After resigning from his civil service job, Richard was encouraged by a friend to go to a truck driving school to become a semi-truck driver. According to his friend, semi-truck drivers were in high demand across the country, and the pay was good. So he enrolled in a six month's driving course held at Washington Homes Vocational Tech in Chipley, Florida.

Richard had no problem passing the course and soon was in possession of his commercial license. He then took a position as a driver for Poole Truck Line, which was headquartered in Evergreen, Alabama. They had a substation in the Pensacola area, which enabled Richard to operate out of a home base. His territory was the southeast quadrant of the United States. His starting salary, which was a significant drop from his ending civil service pay, was $400 a month.

Richard was energized by the challenges associated with driving an eighteen-wheeler. He became very adept at maneuvering the big rig in tight situations. And he usually enjoyed conversing with the loading and unloading crews at the various delivery stops he made. He would pick their brains for credible information regarding delivery times, best eating places, current weather info, etc.

One thing Richard abhorred was helping unload the cargo he was delivering. However, a number of stops expected it—one in particular. His stint in the marine corps dealing with several men under his command had taught him to be creative in achieving his goals.

After much contemplation, he devised an ingenious plan. When he had a delivery to make to the unloading dock in question, he would sweet-talk the young lady who was in charge of filling out the bill of lading to specifically designate that the cargo was to be unloaded by the receiving facility.

So with the revised bill of lading in hand for the designated stop, Richard was grinning from ear to ear. After he had backed up to the unloading dock, he enthusiastically presented the bill of lading to the supervisor in charge. After the supervisor glanced over the bill of lading, he turned to Richard and told him to get busy unloading the cargo.

With a smirk on his face Richard announced, "I don't have to!"

"Oh yes, you do, you smart-ass!"

"No, I don't!"

"Don't get smart with me, you wimp!"

"You'd best read the first paragraph of the bill of lading."

After several seconds had passed, he looked at Richard in utter disgust. "Why you—!"

"Hey, if you've got a problem, call the supplier!" Although pay-backs are usually hell to deal with, it didn't bother Richard.

In order to get revenge, a few deliveries later, the supervisor screwed around for several hours before he would have the cargo unloaded. Ironically, Richard enjoyed the break; it gave him ample time to catch up on his sleep.

Even though he was an excellent, safety-conscious driver for the company, he didn't like the long hours which kept him away from his family. When a position as a dispatcher opened up, he applied for it and was awarded the job. Richard wasn't pleased with the cut in pay from $400 to $300 a week, but he appreciated being able to spend more time with his family.

Once again, Richard's military experience served him well as a dispatcher for Poole Truck Line. Directing and assigning the company's truck drivers was right down his alley. Much to the consternation of some of the older drivers, he didn't play favorites. He prided himself on efficiency and fairness. When a delivery needed to be made, he assigned the load to the driver who was immediately available.

Three months into his new position as dispatcher, he discovered that a form of nepotism was prevalent in the company. On a Monday morning, his boss called him on the "carpet."

"Mr. Warner!"

"Yes, sir, what can I do for you?"

"Well, I'm hearing complaints from some of our senior drivers that you assign some of their deliveries to other drivers."

"Yes, sir, I do. I don't believe we need to wait a day or two to have a load delivered. And the receiving companies seem to appreciate the timeliness of our deliveries."

"Besides the point, Mr. Warner! You will apologize to the drivers. Just tell them you were unaware of your oversight and the way things are supposed to operate."

"But—""

"Don't interrupt me! Get the job done!"

"Yes, sir!"

The next morning, Richard turned in his resignation and gathered up his personal belongings and left.

"Do your job well, have high expectations for yourself and others, and be fair in your dealings with all people," was a motto that was engraved into him from an early age.

Lady luck seemed to be smiling down on him as he caught wind of an opening with a reputable trucking outfit, Puritan Bennett Company, which was headquartered in Lenexa, Kansas.

41

BACK IN THE SADDLE AGAIN

The Puritan Bennett Company was a huge trucking firm. Their territory encompassed the East Coast to the West Coast of the United States and from the Canadian border to the Mexican border. The company's answer to the long drives their drivers would have to endure was the utilization of the team driving concept, which worked very well and which their driver safety rating would attest to. The Puritan truck firm employed two driving scenarios: (1) the two drivers would exchange driving duties every five hours, or (2) they would work on eight-hour shifts. Interestingly enough, this team driving idea was the hardest thing for Richard to get used to doing, as he much preferred driving solo.

The company's primary choice in trucks was the Kenworth, which was noted for its longevity and mechanical soundness.

Richard usually enjoyed the long hauls as he got to view America's varied and beautiful scenery. The downside to these trips was obviously the prolonged separation from his family.

In the seven years, 1986–993, that he worked for the Puritan Bennett trucking firm, he only had to deal with two accidents—both were nonhuman related, and he was the driver both times. On one occasion, an owl hit the right side of the windshield. The unusual aspect of this hit was that the force of it left a perfectly cracked circle on the windshield.

At around midnight on another long-distance haul, a large deer bolted out of the road ditch and was crunched by the left front fender of the semi. The impact of the blow knocked the fender into the tire. Richard and his team driver had to use a cheater bar to pry the fender loose from the tire.

The other possible incidents that could have occurred over this seven-year stretch were fortunately avoided. One evening near the end of his eight-hour shift, Richard began to doze off as his rig headed for the shoulder of the road. After the semi began leaving the pavement, he was suddenly awakened out of his stupor. Thankfully his driving skills acquired over several years of driving came into play, and he was able to avoid jackknifing the rig. His team driver was rudely awakened by the commotion and demanded to know, "What the hell is going on!"

"Oh, just a driver almost losing control," he replied, which was actually the truth.

During the winter season of '87, Richard had the morning driving shift. He was operating the rig heading to Denver, Colorado, on I-70 from Western Kansas. Weather information on the radio as well as CB transmissions from other truckers warned of snowy, windy conditions between Limon and Denver. West of Limon near Deer Trail, he encountered white-out conditions that resulted in a white-knuckled 30 mph trek for several miles. Ironically his biographer was driving a greyhound meat delivery truck for Triple A Brand Company and was heading back east to Burlington, Colorado. He was forced to stay over in Limon for the rest of the day.

The weather finally began to clear as Richard worked his way north of Denver on I-25 heading for Wyoming. When his driving teammate awoke, he wanted to know why they weren't well on their way into Wyoming. Richard carefully explained the scary driving conditions he had just maneuvered though on I-70 east of Denver. To this day, he's not so sure his team driver believes him, as he accused Richard of making an unscheduled truck stop.

A story several of the drivers liked to banter around at truck stops involved a couple of neophyte drivers for J. B. Hunt Trucking. This was a very large trucking firm headquartered in Arkansas. According to the story, these two drivers had made a scheduled stop at the largest and most popular truck stop in Gallup, New Mexico.

This truck stop had everything—it was like a small city. There were medical and dental facilities, a grocery store, several restaurants, motel accommodations, and shops catering to most needs.

After fueling their semi, the codriver went to use the restroom facilities while the driver remained with the truck. Before returning to the rig the codriver decided to pick up some snacks. As he was preparing to pay for the snacks, he noticed some shiny containers up on the shelf behind the checkout lady.

"Ma'am, what are those shiny things on the shelf behind you?"

"Why, those are Thermos jugs."

"And what's so cool about that?"

"Well, they keep hot stuff like soup hot and cold stuff like ice-tea cold."

When he returned to the truck with his goodies, the driver questioned him on why it took him so long. He explained about his purchase of the thermos jug.

"What's the big deal? What's so special about it?"

"Well, it will keep hot things hot and cold things cold."

"So what did you get to put into the jug?"

"I've got some chicken noodle soup in it and some ice-tea in it!"

Unfortunately, during these years of prolonged hauls across the country, Richard's family situation would begin to unravel.

42

DEALING WITH FAMILY

During his seven years with the Puritan trucking company, things were very hectic on the home front. Their son, Devin, graduated with highest academic honors from the University of West Florida with a business degree. He had a perfect 4.0 grade point average all four years and was acknowledged on graduation day as being the first student from the university to achieve that distinction. Following his graduation, he took a job with the Shell Oil Company in Houston, Texas.

Daree, on the other hand, decided to pursue her dreams at the American Academy of Dramatic Arts in Pasadena, California. At the academy she met and became friends with Melissa Gilbert, who would later star in the popular TV series *Little House on the Prairie*. Daree had her own vehicle, and she would often drive Melissa around to various activities and appointments.

The huge earthquake in Southern California would scare Daree and her brother, Devin, who was working in the area at that time, back home to Pensacola. A short time later, Daree landed a job at Disney World in Orlando.

In the meantime, Druwanda was busy helping their children with their moves and also looking after Richard's mother and her ailing parents.

After Richard's father had passed away from a heart attack in the early '60s, his mother later married a navy chief, Robert Brooker in 1965. Even though she would have preferred to stay in DC, she and her second husband purchased a house in Ormond Beach, Florida, in 1983. Following five years of retired bliss, Robert was killed while riding on a moped in 1989. At the time of his death, he had been married to Richard's mother twenty-four years—ironically the same number of years that she had been to Mr. Warner at the time of his heart attack.

Richard's mother stayed in the house at Ormond Beach for another year. Because of her declining health, Richard purchased a home for her in 1990. It was located two blocks down the street from their home. In less than six months, because of a fall his mother had sustained, they moved her into their home. And about that time, they also moved Druwanda's parents in with them because of their health issues.

It was during these years that Richard began to increasingly feel shunned by Druwanda in his need for her attention. She had moved out of their bedroom into another bedroom because of his incessant snoring, which he disputed. To prove her point to him, she secretly recorded his snoring one evening. When she confronted him with the irrefutable evidence, he was red-faced with amazement. The snoring was very loud and disgusting.

Richard was aware that his wife and their daughter Daree were very close. In fact, one Christmas holiday, Druwanda informed him that she and her mother were going to visit Daree in Orlando. He was dismayed that she hadn't asked him to go along with her. Instead, he had to stay behind and keep tabs on her father and his mother. It always appeared to him like it was his wife, daughter, and her mother who were enjoying themselves at his expense.

Unfortunately, these feelings of neglect would continue to fester within his psyche.

And to compound matters, his beloved mother would soon pass away from a fall she sustained in a nursing home.

43

S—— Hits the Fan!

Due to the alienation Richard was sensing with his family and the extra burden of caring for their ailing parents, he ended his seven-year employment with the Puritan Bennett Company's trucking firm.

Shortly thereafter, his mother's passing was devastating to him. Throughout his life, she was his Rock of Gibraltar, his guiding light. Now he felt like his back was up against the wall and no one was in his corner.

To honor his mother's memory, he felt it was his duty to return pictures and personal items of hers that were of a nonfamily nature. During this trying time, Druwanda was an angel. She took it upon herself to sort all his mother's belongings into designated piles. When she was finished, Richard decided to personally deliver the respective items to those persons he felt should have them.

He asked Druwanda to take a trip with him up the East Coast to deliver the goods. However, she declined the invitation. He was hoping for some reconciliation of their current marital situation.

After loading his mother's personal belongings, he headed out. It was a mission he believed he owed his mother. He enjoyed visiting with some of his mother's former students and some of the teachers who worked for her in her private school, as well as some of her best friends. Their sincere sympathies were very gratifying to him.

Thanks to all his truck driving excursions, he knew the value of maps to get him to his destination. And, Rand McNally was the atlas of his choice. However, on his way through Maryland he stopped at a very small town called Deal that sported its own post office. He couldn't find the small town listed on the map of Maryland. Later, when he returned back to Florida, he wrote to the Rand McNally Company, alerting them concerning their oversight on omitting the town of Deal from their map of Maryland. In a few weeks, he received a thank-you note from the company. They apologized for their omission of Deal from the map of Maryland. When their Atlas was updated, they sent him a complimentary copy of it.

One of his final deliveries was to Jacqueline Lamson in Hackensack, New Jersey. They had attended high school together, and her sister had taught in his mother's private school. He would have liked to have dated her in high school, but her mother was 100 percent against her daughter dating any boys at the time.

Richard and Jacqueline recognized each other as soon as she answered the door. He explained his mission on his mother's behalf and handed her a small box of mementos. She informed him of her recent loss of her husband, and they continued to exchange pleasantries regarding their past years.

"Oh, forgive me," she said, "would you please come in and let me get you something to drink?"

"That would be fine. I'd appreciate it!" he enthused.

The next morning, he returned to Florida. He was feeling better. He had found an old acquaintance whom he felt at ease conversing with.

Following his return home, he went to the local post office and rented a box in his name. He then wrote a nice long thank-you letter to Jacqueline with the PO box number highlighted. A written correspondence soon ensued between the two of them. Needless to say, Druwanda discovered a name and address on a slip of paper that he had inadvertently left in a coat pocket. When confronted with the evidence, he couldn't deny it. She informed him that she had contacted a law firm and was going to formally begin divorce proceedings. Ironically he had filed for divorce a year before. Much to his consternation, the fee he wound up paying the law firm was a whopping $10,000!

In March of 1995, Richard purchased a freightliner semi-truck from an ex-marine for a sales price of $20,000. On his first trip to

Fargo, North Dakota, he was disappointed in the truck's performance. It seemed to be seriously lacking in power. When he returned to Orlando, he had a mechanic friend of his check the engine out. The news wasn't too good. It needed a complete overhaul to the tune of $6,000. In addition, his mechanic discovered thousands upon thousands of fire ants located under the "dog house" cover that was situated between the driver's seat and the passenger's seat above the engine.

While his truck was being overhauled, Richard purchased a '95 GMC Safari van. In a pullout tray located under the passenger seat, he kept the urn that contained the cremated ashes of his mother. He also had a phone installed in the van.

Richard's sister, Betty, lived in Glendale Springs, North Carolina. His sister was well-acquainted with Jacqueline and had her come for a visit. Richard then drove to Betty's place to see her. While there, he and Betty took their mother's ashes to the New River, which was close by. He deemed this an appropriate place to spread her ashes. The New River was the only river on the East Coast that flowed in a northerly direction. So in a sense, he felt he was sending his mother home. He performed what he thought was a fitting Christian prayer service for her.

Later at his sister's home, he was able to get in contact with Jacqueline at her twin sister's home in Maryland.

"Hello?"

"Jacqueline, how would you like to move to Florida?"

"I'd love too, if you'll come and get me," she gushed.

"I'm on my way!"

In less than a week, Richard had moved Jacqueline into an apartment in Orlando, Florida. In a matter of days, he presented her with an engagement ring, which she accepted.

During this period of time, he and Druwanda met four times in an attempt at reconciliation. At their last try to mend fences Druwanda asked Richard to go to a nearby bakery and pick up some doughnuts. However, he left and never returned.

In June of 1995, Richard and Druwanda's divorce was finalized. She retained possession of all their properties. Apparently as a gesture of good faith, he presented her with a brand-new Buick car.

Richard couldn't help but feel years later that their lawyers played a large role in the culmination of their divorce.

To paraphrase a famous movie quote, "What we have here is a failure to communicate."

44

LIFE GOES ON

After Richard's truck was repaired and running satisfactorily, he resumed hauling freight across the country. One haul took him to Denver, Colorado, where he unloaded his cargo, and then he headed south on I-25 to pick up a load of potatoes. He got off on the Walsenburg exit and took Highway 160 west over La Veta Pass to the San Luis Valley. When he got to Monte Vista, he headed north to Sargent to pick up his load from a potato warehouse. He enjoyed the mountain scenery as the San Luis Valley is surrounded by mountains on all sides. The San Luis Valley is also the highest alpine valley in the world. A few days later, he successfully delivered the potatoes to a large grocery store chain in Florida.

At this time, his relationship with Jacqueline, although pleasant and cordial, was somewhat static. They enjoyed eating out, going to movies, and visiting interesting places. However, it was evident that Richard was still confronting his personal demons.

Richard had rented an apartment in a large building complex in the Pensacola area. He would travel three to four times a week to visit with Jacqueline in Orlando. Also during this time, he made several attempts to visit with or communicate with his children, Devin and Daree. He came up empty handed every time.

In early 1996, Richard and Jacqueline split as their relationship, although friendly, was apparently going nowhere. She returned to her home in New Jersey.

While on a freight haul in Connecticut in August of 1996, Richard was stricken with a heart attack at a truck stop. (This was outlined in the opening chapter of this biography.)

A week after the heart surgery, he was dismissed from the hospital, and he returned to his apartment in Pensacola. When he arrived at the apartment, he had to spend a very painful night trying to get some rest on the floor. In his absence, Druwanda had cleared all the furniture out of the place. The next morning, he made arrangements to get a bed and mattress delivered to the apartment.

Realizing his semi-truck driving days were over, Richard contacted a cousin of his, Billy Spaar, and hired him to tow his truck, which was still in Connecticut, to his farm. He asked Billy to then go ahead and try to sell the truck for him. A few weeks later Billy gave him a call:

"Hey, Richard, this is Cousin Billy."

"Yes, Billy, what do you know?"

"I've got a potential buyer for your truck."

"Did he make an offer?"

"Yes, he did, but only for $11,000. And it's the best offer I've gotten."

"I hate to sell it for that price, but you better go ahead with it."

"Okay, Richard," Billy said, "but it's too bad because your truck is one of the cleanest and most well-maintained used semis that I've ever seen!"

"Thanks, Billy, I really appreciate your help."

Richard was in a limbo; he wasn't sure what the next day held in store for him. And several months of rehab lie ahead.

45

A NEW BEGINNING PERHAPS?

In December 1998, Richard was taking some excess magazines that he had accumulated to the apartment complex's laundromat. As he headed across the courtyard, he spotted a lovely lady standing on a second-story balcony of an apartment opposite his. He had been aware of her presence there before.

"Good morning, ma'am," he called out, "it's a beautiful day, isn't it!"

"And, a good morning to you, sir! Yes, it is a beautiful morning," she said in her German accent. "What are you carrying there?"

"Why, just a bunch of old magazines that I had. I'm taking them to the laundromat for people to read while they're doing their laundry."

"That's very nice of you," she replied.

"Excuse me, ma'am, I forgot to introduce myself. I'm Richard Warner."

"And I'm Erika Roszak."

"Pleased to make your acquaintance, ma'am!"

"Likewise. What do you do, Mr. Warner?"

"I'm a retired marine corps veteran, and I'm currently recovering from a heart attack I suffered while driving a semi-truck."

"Oh, I'm sorry to hear that."

"That's okay. By the way, what are you doing here in Florida?"

"I'm here for a couple of months visiting my son who is an instructor at Pensacola Naval Air Base."

"Say, would you like to go to dinner with me this evening?"

"I would love to!"

"I'll pick you up at 7:00 p.m. I know a good Italian restaurant I think you would enjoy."

"Oh, that would be great! I enjoy Italian food!"

Thus, an enjoyable, friendly relationship ensued between the two of them. They enjoyed eating out, going to movies, and visiting local sights. Richard became Erika's personal chauffeur, which he thoroughly enjoyed doing as he loved their companionship very much. He took her to appointments, church, and shopping. Being a foreigner, she did not have a driver's license.

Erika was well read, and she had a keen interest in exotic and scenic places. One evening she mentioned the desire to see the Redwood Forest in California. So in a matter of days, they were on their way to California. She thanked Richard for taking her to this magnificent sight. She repeatedly said she couldn't believe trees could grow so high.

In November 1999, Erika informed him of her need to return to Germany, a return trip she had actually scheduled the day they met. And she was pleased that he was eager to go with her.

To further impress her, he made a trip to a foreign car dealership in Fort Walton Beach in Florida and ordered a C-230 Kompressor Mercedes-Benz German car to be picked up at the factory in Germany when he and Erika arrived.

Shortly after arriving in Germany, Richard picked up the C-230 Kompressor in a factory located in a suburb of Stuttgart. He then rented a studio apartment from a Dr. Bollig in Garmisch-Partenkirchen (more fondly referred to as GAP) near the Italian border.

Three months later, Erika and Richard returned to the States in February 2000. He had his new German car shipped from Munich to Atlanta, Georgia. From there the car was transported to the dealership in Fort Walton Beach, Florida, where he had ordered the car from.

Once they picked up the car in Florida, they made a trip to New Hampshire. From her readings, Erika thought New Hampshire might be a good place to live, and they had an excellent hospital there. Besides, she wasn't too fond of Florida's humidity or its drinking water.

They decided to take a break after spending a few weeks house hunting and take a trip to Clarksville, Tennessee. Erika was very familiar with the area as she and her former husband had lived there. Her husband was in the military and was stationed at Fort Campbell, Kentucky, which was close to Clarksville. A few years later, he died suddenly on deployment in Germany. In compliance with his wishes, he was buried in the National Cemetery in Nancy, Kentucky. Several Civil War soldiers are also interred there. She wished to place some flowers on his grave site.

Because Erika was familiar with and at ease with Clarksville, they decided to purchase a home there. In a few days, they found a house to their liking. It was owned by a German lady, and the interior was absolutely impeccable.

The next six years for Richard were retirement bliss. He and Erika found great contentment in tending to their spacious garden and yard. And they spent three months a year enjoying the climate and sights of Germany. Richard had rented the spacious studio apartment from Dr. Bollig on a year-round basis. He spent hours touring the countryside on his bicycle.

Back at home in Clarksville, he would also take Erika on travels to the far reaches of the country, from Nova Scotia to Key West and to the rain forest in Washington State. And two or three times a year, they would pay their respects with flowers to Erika's husband's burial plot in the National Cemetery in Nancy, Kentucky.

The winds of change in the fall of 2006 were about to disrupt the rosy arrangement between the two of them. One afternoon, Richard was wrestling with a stubborn tree stump that he was trying to dislodge from the flower garden. Exhausted, he fell to the ground as his heart went into fibrillation. He felt like he was being hit by a heart attack again. It would be determined later that he was woefully low on potassium. Fortunately, Erika was close by and went into the house and called for immediate medical help.

One of the interns who initially checked Richard's vital signs declared, "Hey, this old dude is DOA [dead on arrival]!"

A second intern, also doing a quick observation, confirmed the first intern's diagnosis, "I believe you're right. The old geezer is a goner!"

Fortunately, a more thorough examination revealed there was still hope. Interestingly enough, Richard was aware of the circumstances and the conversations that were going on around him.

On the eighteenth of June 2006, Dr. Petrascik successfully replaced the mitral value in Richard's heart at Vanderbilt Hospital in Nashville, Tennessee.

Erika, who was shocked by these events, was also having health issues of her own. She had been battling a chronic cough for months, which she blamed on the time that she had spent in Florida. To combat this persistent health problem, she felt it necessary to return to Germany.

After informing Richard of her decision, she departed for Germany.

46

WORLD UPSIDE DOWN—AGAIN!

Much to Richard's dismay, Erika took all her belongings, pictures, clothing, and personal items back with her to Germany. She apparently wasn't anticipating a quick return to Clarksville.

In the meantime, as Richard was working through his rehab period, he became friendly with a German lady whom he had met before at a German bakery shop. Her official name was Ot.tillie Bain, better known to her friends as Sweet Mary. She invited him to a Christmas party in December 2006 at a local Catholic church.

They started dating once a week by attending a German club and met regularly at a nearby Mexican restaurant. About a year later, he invited her to his home. The biggest problem he had with her was that she was a smoker. Shortly after they arrived at his place, she started to light up a cigarette.

"Oh no, you don't!" he cautioned her. "You will not smoke in my house!"

"Well, you're an old stick-in-the-mud," she retorted. "How about if I just step outside and light up?"

"No way!"

"You don't have to get so uppity about it! I'm going around the back of the house so no one will see me!"

"Listen, Sweet Mary, you will not smoke in my house or on my property! If you insist, that will break up our relationship!"

"Okay, but you're a real pain!"

In October 2007, on her second visit to his home, Sweet Mary informed him that she felt uncomfortable being in the house when Erika was unaware of it, so she demanded he call her and explain their relationship to her.

Much to his chagrin, he conceded and made a call to Erika in Germany. It was the first time they had spoken in over a year. Needless to say, Erika was distraught with the news. And he was disgusted with himself for allowing Sweet Mary to back him in a corner to make the call.

Richard became very despondent over the next couple of years, and although he continued to see Sweet Mary, he missed Erica's presence. This was evident as the upkeep necessary to maintaining a warm and loving home went to pot. The place, inside and out, was a mess.

During this troubled time, he did keep in contact with Erika's son Chris, who was living in Colorado Springs, Colorado. Chris informed Richard that he had rented an apartment for his mother there, and he was expecting her to arrive in February 2010.

After she arrived in Colorado Springs, Richard called her and talked her into coming back to Clarksville. Once she agreed to his pleading for her return, he immediately ended his friendship with Sweet Mary.

Erika was in total shock when she entered their home—it was filthy!

"How could you do this?" she demanded.

"Uh, I missed you so much, I guess I let things go."

"You can say that again!"

"I'm sorry, it's my fault."

In the next six to seven months, Erika applied a great deal of elbow grease and effort into getting the home into a livable condition again. Richard tried to appease her by working hard making the yard and gardens into presentable shape.

In October, Richard decided to test the housing market by putting their house up for sale. The real estate agent warned him that the housing market was soft and that the properties in their area were being priced at around $100,000. He instructed the real estate agent to market the house at $125,000, assuming that there would probably be no takers. However, two days later the house sold.

They were surprised the house sold, but they were pleased with the sales price. They decided to journey to Sarasota, Florida, in November 2010 and look for a place to live. Erika picked out an apartment in a large complex of apartments that was to her liking.

They returned to Clarksville, loaded up their belongings, and moved to Sarasota in December 2010. Accompanying them on their move was Ericka's calico cat.

In late December, Erika informed Richard of her need to return to Germany. Shortly before her departure she told him there was going to be an empty seat next to hers on the plane. Unfortunately, he declined the offer.

47

ON THE MOVE AGAIN

Instead of moping around following Erika's departure for Germany, Richard decided to get on with his life and look for gainful employment. It didn't take long in his search to find a job. He met an enterprising lady, Jo Anne Fry, who ran a very successful delivery business called Executive Express Courier. This was an exclusive delivery service that catered to banks, medical facilities, large construction companies, etc. They delivered and picked up important documents, money, or sealed bids—in the case of the construction companies. Richard thoroughly enjoyed the responsibility and trust involved as a driver for the courier service. And his boss, Jo Anne Fry, was impressed with his dedication and professionalism.

In February 2012, after several frustrating attempts to reach Erika in Germany, Richard decided to contact her son, Chris, in Colorado Springs again. He learned from him that Erika was in a hospital having a cancerous kidney removed. Additional health issues would soon plague Richard again. A good friend of his advised him, because of his age, to have his prostrate checked by a urologist. During the routine examination, several small polyps were discovered. These were removed and sent to a lab at John Hopkins Hospital in Maryland.

Ten days later, he met with Dr. Winston Barze II to find out the results of the lab tests.

"Well, Doc, good news or bad news?"

"I'm afraid it's not good news. The results of the lab tests indicate that you have an aggressive form of cancer."

"What can we do?"

"There are two or three options that we can pursue. We can do surgery, chemotherapy, or radiation."

"What would you recommend?"

"I would recommend attacking it with radiation treatments. I know this is devastating news for you, so take a few days and think it over."

Richard was of a mind-set to get it over with as quickly as possible—the sooner, the better. So at this point in time, he was leaning toward surgery, but, he thought it best to seek a second opinion. He got an appointment to see Dr. Pow-sang, a noted Peruvian doctor at Moffitt Cancer Center in Tampa, Florida. Dr. Pow-sang was in 100 percent agreement with Dr. Barzell's recommendations for treatment. Both doctors also told him that his heart condition would never withstand a surgical procedure.

In January 2013, he began a series of forty radiation treatments that were administered on a daily basis. Around this same time Erika's son Chris called Richard and told him that he had located a nice house for him in Colorado Springs if he was still interested in purchasing property there.

After receiving twenty-five treatments, he informed Dr. Barzell of his intention to move to Colorado Springs. Dr. Bayell, who owned a home in Aspen, Colorado, told him he knew one of the best doctors in the country who he could continue his treatments with. He referred him to Dr. E. David Crawford in Aurora, Colorado, a suburb of Denver.

Richard headed for Colorado Springs on March 15, 2013. Before he left, Dr. Barzell injected him with a shot that imbedded radiation seeds into the affected area. Dr. Crawford repeated this procedure every three months. After the third time, he told Richard he was a miracle case and that his cancer was in full remission. In March 2014, Dr. Crawford said that he only needed to return every three months for a checkup.

With this good prognosis in hand, Richard decided to look for a part-time delivery job. In late November 2014, while he was having his Mercedes-Benz serviced at Salin Silver Star Service, his mechanic introduced him to Geoff Dunbar, who had a contract to deliver lost luggage bags for several airlines. Geoff was impressed with Richard's driving background and hired him to help deliver lost luggage, primarily in the southeast quadrant of Colorado. Since January of 2015, he has logged over forty thousand miles delivering lost luggage.

Erika returned to Colorado Springs in September 2015 and is currently residing with her son. At this time all Richard's attempts to contact her have failed.

48

DELIVERING LOST AIRPLANE LUGGAGE

At eighty-one years of age, Richard insists on keeping active, although he is constantly battling several health issues. Much of his week is devoted to combating those health problems and trying to get in some workout routines. His weekends are taken up with delivering lost airplane luggage to area owners. He drives from his residence to the Colorado Springs Airport to pick up his fare for the day. Once he has his delivery sheet in hand, he then enters the addresses into his cell phone's GPS system, and then he proceeds to make his deliveries in an orderly fashion. Several years of driving a semi-truck made this a good option for him. The pay per delivered suitcase is minimal, so he depends on tips for spending money, but he enjoys meeting people and the scenery of the mountainous terrain.

The first obstacle he must deal with is Mother Nature. Richard's primary territory encompasses South Central and South Eastern Colorado, with occasional forays in the Denver area. Because of the unpredictability of the Colorado weather, he might be driving at any one given time through a downpour of rain, various sizes of hail, extreme winds, ice, and snow. The most difficult conditions to deal with for him are snow whiteouts and dense fog. The inherent problems are disorientation and careless drivers.

Because of his vast driving experience all over the country, Richard finds the traffic on weekends to be basically minimal. Exceptions are occasionally the drive to Denver from the Springs on I-25 due to an accident causing a huge backup of vehicles. Sometimes the rural country roads can be a problem, especially if rain has caused washout conditions. Of course, snow-covered passes and roads can also present problems.

Richard has had very little problems with animals in all the miles he has driven delivering suitcases. In fact, he looks forward to seeing all kinds of critters. Once near the airport on his way to pick up the lost luggage, he counted forty-nine antelope. On another occasion, he stopped and took picture of an elk herd in the mountains. On a delivery in the Kissing Camels region northeast of Colorado Springs, he spotted several deer.

Other than occasional bad weather to cope with, people can sometimes be a real headache. Ironically, the rudest and least likely to leave a tip are the wealthiest people. One such incident involved a high-ranking NCO at one of the local military establishments. This individual was not only very rude but used a stream of unprintable curse words. Richard was prompted to write a letter of reprimand to the base commander. However, many of the people are kind and generous. On a couple of different outings, he has been helped out of difficult road conditions.

Here is an actual example of a recent typical week for Richard:

While loading the lost luggage fare for the day, he stumbled and fell trying to load a heavy backpack. Richard complained that it felt like it was loaded with a bunch of heavy rocks. After delivering the backpack to a senior NCO at Fort Carson, he questioned him as to the content of said backpack. He informed Richard that he and his wife had just recently returned from a vacation in Scotland, and one of the popular outdoor sports in Scotland is the throwing of large rounded stones—akin to our throwing of the shotput. The souvenir stone he brought back weighed twenty-three pounds, in addition to all the other personal items they had stuffed into it.

Later that same night, he was called upon to deliver a suitcase to a woman in Victor, Colorado, at a location of ten thousand feet above sea level. He returned home at around midnight.

Richard was up at six the next morning to make preparations for his trip to his doctor's office to have his INR checked. It was at a level of 1.2. He was advised to stop taking Warfarin on Wednesday

to get ready to switch to Pradaxa. Hopefully it will be a big improvement for him if his body can tolerate a new drug in his system. He
took the first 150 mg the next morning and the second one in the
evening—a twelve=hour spread.

Then Richard went in for his radiation treatment for two basil
cell carcinoma s on his face—one was located behind his left ear and
the other one close to his left eye.

Early on Saturday morning of that week, he got up at four to
deliver two containers of musical instruments to a couple of guys
who were performing in a Bluegrass Festival being held in Westcliffe,
Colorado. Both of the young men were very appreciative of Richard's
effort in getting their instruments to them. In fact, they invited him
to stay and hear them play. Unfortunately, he had to return to the
Colorado Springs Airport for his one o'clock sweep.

But it's so much fun!

49

My Two Cents' Worth

Richard's current medical status is a daunting one. In 1996, he suffered a severe heart attack at a truck stop in Branford, Connecticut, after an eighteen-hour stint driving a semi- truck. And several severe health issues have plagued him ever since.

He had his fourth pacemaker installed in his chest in February 2017, at Memorial Hospital in Colorado Springs. He jokingly compared the procedure to getting an oil change.

He has been diagnosed as a type 2 diabetic and must take two insulin shots per day.

Three years ago, he had cataract surgery that was so successful he no longer wears glasses.

It was also determined that he suffers from COPD (chronic obstructive pulmonary disease) as his lungs were functioning at only 60 percent capacity.

And most recently, he has undergone radiation treatments for some basil carcinomas on his nose, face, neck, and back.

He remains an eternal optimist: "All I need is some fresh air and eight hours of sleep!"

Richard believes one of our most serious problems in our country today revolves around the liberal left's attempt to turn our Christian-based society into a secular one. The concept that is being purported is that everyone is a victim and that everything is someone else's fault. Everyone is entitled. He urges everyone to listen to Paul Harvey's 1965 radio broadcast entitled *If I Were the Devil*. Richard became a born-again Christian several years ago at a Southern Baptist Church.

Richard believes the number 1 problem in our educational system is a lack of discipline among the students and faculty. He also believes we must do away with trying every new fix-it-all strategy that comes along such as the current core curriculum. And we must return to teaching history as it should be taught instead of the socialists' attempt to rewrite it in their favor. Surprisingly, he sees technology as a plus for our educational system.

He also believes our legal system needs serious revamping. It's discouraging when you realize our country contains 5 percent of the world's population and 67 percent of the lawyers.

Richard strongly believes our mass media is a total disgrace to the world. They are trying to create the news instead of actually trying to report it. They are hell-bent on a socialist agenda.

And he believes we must back our police force or suffer the consequences. It's a disgrace that the liberal left portrays them as the bad guys.

Being a retired marine, Richard strongly believes in a strong fighting force. He believes our current administration is on the right path to rectify many of our current domestic and foreign problems.

Semper Fi! I may smell like bacon, but I haven't oinked yet!

50

A Latent Dream Fulfilled

Encouraged by a biography written about his famous uncle J. Allen Crocker, which was entitled *Technocrat*, Richard secretly hoped that someday a biography could be written that detailed his life's trials, tribulations, and successes. Besides, his dad, Dr. Warner, was a published author of several educational texts. When he discovered that his oldest sister's daughter, Judy Cook, was an excellent writer in her own right, he tried to entice her into doing his biography for him. She flat-out denied his request.

On a Wednesday morning, prior to getting a call to deliver lost luggage, he decided to eat breakfast at a Village Inn restaurant on East Woodman Road. His choice of selecting Village Inn for breakfast this day was primarily because they offered a free slice of a fruit pie as an enticement to eat at their establishment.

At seven thirty in the morning, the place was only sparsely filled with customers. As he waited for a waitress to seat him, he noticed off to his right an elderly gentleman who was occupying a booth by himself. When the waitress asked him if he was ready to be seated, he told her that if it was okay with her, he'd go over and see if he could sit with the gentleman he pointed out to her. She told him to go for it.

"Excuse me, sir, is anyone seating with you?"

"Uh, why no, there isn't. Be my guest."

"Thank you. Sorry to interrupt, I hope you don't mind some company."

"Oh no, I'm just waiting for my order to come."

After giving his breakfast order to the waitress, Richard introduced himself.

"I forgot to introduce myself. I'm Richard Warner."

"I'm Galen Conrardy. I couldn't help but notice your military cap. Are you a retired marine?"

"Well, in a way, I served twelve years in the navy and the marine corps. I've also driven a semi-truck for several years, had a government civil service job, and I sold insurance, amongst other things. How about you? I noticed you have a military cap on too?"

"I served six years in the Colorado and Kansas Army National Guard during the Vietnam War. Fortunately, my unit was never deployed there. Are you a native of the Springs?"

"Oh no, I've been here only about two years. I guess you could say I'm semi-retired. I deliver lost luggage a couple of days a week. How about you? What do you do?"

"I'm a retired teacher/coach. I've been retired for the past five years. My wife still works for Farm Credit of Southern Colorado here in the Springs. She's almost seven years younger than I am. She plans on retiring next March. We've been here in the Springs almost nineteen years."

"What did you teach and coach?"

"I taught language arts courses, writing, journalism, drama, etc., primarily on the high school level. Coached football, basketball, baseball, and track."

"Wow! What do you do now that you are retired?"

"Well, I make breakfast and dinner for my wife during the week when she is working. I also do dishes, laundry, house cleaning, some babysitting, and yard work. And after procrastinating for over two years, I've finally got back to doing some writing."

"Man, you're one busy character! But I'm impressed with what you just said—that you're a writer?"

"Yes, I am. I'm a published author. I wrote a book about growing up with my younger brother on a farm in Western Kansas called *Growing Up with Roy.*"

"That's fantastic! You know I've always wanted a book written about my life. You wouldn't be interested in writing about my life, would you?"

"I don't know, I'm pretty busy with my own writing right now. I'd have to think about it."

"Oh, I would sure appreciate it if you would at least consider it. And if you do decide to, for whatever reason, I only have one request concerning the book."

"And, what would that be?"

"I'm very adamant about this. The title of my biography must be, *I May Smell like Bacon, but I Haven't Oinked yet!*"

"Are you kidding me?"

"No, I'm not. If you should be possibly interested in writing it, let's meet again next week same time and discuss it further."

"I'll tell you what, I will meet with you here next Wednesday. If nothing else, I want to hear about the smelling-like-bacon thing."

"Thank you, Mr. Conrardy, I'll see you next Wednesday."

The rest of the story appears to be history.

ABOUT THE AUTHOR

A retired teacher, coach, and writer, Galen B. Conrardy has written his youthful autobiography, Growing Up with Roy. In addition to this biography he is currently about to have his first fictional novel published.

CPSIA information can be obtained
at www.ICGtesting.com
Printed in the USA
BVHW041144051122
650897BV00002B/8